I AM COMING—

HEAR MY VOICE!

**Word of the Lord Given to the
World and the Church**

BY SHIRLEY SMITH

"Surely the LORD GOD will do nothing,
but he revealeth his secret unto his
servants the prophets."

■ Amos 3:7

All Scripture quotations, unless indicated otherwise, are from the Holy Bible, New International
Version. Copyright 1973, 1978, 1984 International Bible Society. Used by permission of Zondervan
Bible Publishers.
Spirit-Led Publishing
ISBN 978-1-943011-06-3
Copyright 2015

INTRODUCTION

I remember as a little girl being conscious of God. I was aware that He was somewhere in the heavens. I grew up with a Christian mother and an atheist father who tried to convince me that there was no God. The more he tried to convince me the more adamant I became to find God. This led to my search for God.

I studied many religions and looked into the occult—all I found was organised chaos. In my heart I knew that there can only be one Creator. Because I could not find peace, I had this inborn desire to find God, the Creator. I've always been very aware of nature—the animals and even the universe because that was my father's passion. I grew up learning about the solar system—I saw the organized design yet I yearned to find the God that Created all of this. Where was the Designer? My father kept telling me that the churches are just a business.

This yearning never died and one day I just gave up on my search and went out into my garden and called out to God: "Please help me, I can't find You!" God heard my call and led me straight to Him. So began my journey with the Lord. I then discovered that the Lord speaks to His children just like a physical father and this is what I wanted more than anything—to hear the Lord's voice.

Soon after I got saved, an evangelist came to South Africa and one evening he asked people to come up and ask God for something. I didn't move but he suddenly looked over at me and called me to come forward. He asked me what I wanted and I told him—"to hear the voice of God."

He looked at me with shock on his face and replied, "You know I have never been asked that before but if that's what you want then let's ask God." He prayed over me and I felt the power of God flow through me. My relationship with the Lord grew from that day into a very close bond as the Holy Spirit began teaching me to hear His voice. Some years later a minister from America called me out of a crowd and said: "Rivers of living water are going to flow through you." He repeated the same phrase five times. Then fifteen years ago the Lord led me during prayer that He had a 'task' for me to do and asked me if I would do it. I made a vow to the Lord and said I would, even though I did not know what that 'task' was.

I am involved in Christian counselling and deliverance ministry but I also had my own business, however in June, 2011, the Lord began to prompt me to sell it which I promptly did. Then in January, 2012, the Lord kept putting this into my spirit; "I have a lot to tell you" and that "now is the time." Then the Lord began leading me to come before Him every day—to carefully note the date and time and I am to listen carefully and that the time had come to me to fulfil my vow and this is how I received the Lord's word.

Never, ever could I have imagined or thought that this was the 'task' that I had made a vow to the Lord to do. Each morning as I went prepared before the Lord I *never* had a clue about what He was doing or where we would go to in the Bible. As the days passed I realized how serious this word was. Thoughts would cross my mind as I was writing and the Lord answered them and kept reassuring me. I was terrified that I would not hear correctly and the fear of being a false prophet was great as that was something that always kept me checking myself and seeking God for confirmation.

There were days when I realized that His Word would cause controversy and that some would not believe it was the Lord. The Lord said: "Those that know Me, will know that it is I speaking."

The emotions I experienced every day were the Lord's emotions—I could feel His love and compassion—this would flood me with tears. I could feel His patience—this would astound me. I could feel his determination; determination would rise in me. I would suddenly feel confident. But when I felt His anger, I would cringe in fear and cry and become very upset; yet at other times I became angry in agreement with the Lord. I could see my family and friends that do not know God and will not listen. I saw the world—the evil and how lost it is. I could see and feel the destruction that was coming upon the people of the world. My heart would be so painful that at times it was unbearable.

But when the Lord said that He came and hung on the cross and died for the sins of the world, well words cannot even describe how I felt. He died a horrible death for me. This is all I could see—for me, my family and for a world that has forsaken Him. What a price He paid to rescue humanity!
And now He is sending this word of warning to both the world and His church. He is calling out for us to "listen" and "to hear His voice." He is asking us to *look* around us at the signs of the times and to "see" that He is coming soon.

The Lord led me to Amos 3.7 and this showed me clearly that He does nothing without telling His prophets . In the Old Testament God sent Isaiah, Jeremiah, Ezekiel, Daniel and other prophets to bring warning to Israel. Now He is doing the same thing and has given this word of warning to His church and to the world because each and every soul is precious to the Lord—He does not want one single person to perish.

He is calling out to all that will listen to come "now while there is still time and He can still be found." The Lord God Almighty, Creator of the heavens and earth takes issue with the arrogant and the proud. He takes issue with the church that has turned away from her first love and the foundation that He established. The Lord calls the church to repentance—to return to Him—to put Him back on the Throne. The Lord is not pleased with the church and He makes that very clear. He is calling the church to teach that sin separates man from God and thus sin leads to death. He wants us to seek holiness.

He wants His church to return to the five-fold ministry that He established (Ephesians 4)—to become one with each another and with Him. He asks that His church go forward and return to the Great Commission—to seek the lost—to help the poor and weak—to come now as time is short.

Yes, the Lord is angry, but because of His love and compassion, He is calling all to repent. He uses His Word, the Bible, and references the Bible therein to prove that His Word "is the same yesterday, today and forever" (Hebrews 13:8). It never changes and still applies to us, two thousand years later, to this, the last generation before that great and terrible day of His Second Coming. To Christians the Lord says: "Come out of the world—come out of Babylon. Do not participate with the world and do not approve of nor do what the world does. Repent and put on your whole armour of God and join the battle—stand firm. Make sure your lamps are full. Get back into the Bible—the truth and only truth—for you will stand accountable." Most importantly, and above all, I, His Witness, give the Lord God Almighty, Christ Jesus, all the Praise, Honour and Glory for He alone is Worthy. Just as the prophets of the Bible foretold, HE IS COMING and is on the Horizon. He is prepared and ready and He is asking *you* this—HEAR MY VOICE.

Humbly yours in Christ,

Shirley Smith

I AM COMING

HEAR MY VOICE

Psalm 50

"The Mighty One, God, the LORD, speaks and summons the earth from the rising of the sun to the place where it sets. From Zion, perfect in beauty, God shines forth. Our God comes and will not be silent; a fire devours before him, and around him a tempest rages. He summons the heavens above, and the earth, that he may judge his people: 'Gather to me my consecrated ones, who made a covenant with me by sacrifice.' And the heavens proclaim his righteousness, for God himself is judge.

"'**Hear**, O my people, and I will speak, O Israel, and I will testify against you: I am God, your God. I do not rebuke you for your sacrifices or your burnt offerings, which are ever before me. I have no need of a bull from your stall or of goats from your pens, for every animal of the forest is mine, and the cattle on a thousand hills. I know every bird in the mountains, and the creatures of the field are mine. If I were hungry I would not tell you, for the world is mine, and all that is in it. Do I eat the flesh of bulls or drink the blood of goats? Sacrifice thank offerings to God, fulfill your vows to the Most High, and call upon me in the day of trouble; I will deliver you, and you will honor me.'
But to the wicked, God says: 'What right have you to recite my laws or take my covenant on your lips? You hate my instruction and cast my words behind you. When you see a thief, you join with him; you throw in your lot with adulterers.

You use your mouth for evil and harness your tongue to deceit. You speak continually against your brother and slander your own mother's son. These things you have done and I kept silent; you thought I was altogether like you. But I will rebuke you and accuse you to your face. Consider this, you who forget God, or I will tear you to pieces, with none to rescue: he who sacrifices thank offerings honors me, and he prepares the way so that I may show him the salvation of God.'"

NOW, LISTEN CAREFULLY!
LISTEN, FOR IT IS TIME TO LISTEN!
COME NOW WHILE MERCY AND GRACE ABOUND!
LISTEN, PAY ATTENTION!
COME NOW WHILE THERE IS STILL TIME!
SEE, THE TIME IS HERE!
NOW IS THE TIME!

This all began in June of 2011, during prayer time. The Lord kept telling me, "Now is the time." In January, 2012, I was finally free of all my business commitments and I was about to venture out into a new season of my life. I was waiting on the Lord for direction as my husband and I were considering relocating. However, the Lord kept reminding me that "now is the time." I was not sure what the Lord meant. Never in my wildest dreams could I have imagined that this task is what the Lord had planned for me to do.

Sunday, 29 January, 2012, Time: 9:00 a.m.

Then while in prayer on the morning of the 29th of January, 2012, the Lord told me to come to Him every day and spend time with Him as He has a "lot to tell me." He instructed me to hear and write down everything He tells me and ensure that I have the correct date and time and I must mark all the words. The Lord said "it was a great task" and asked me if I "am ready to do this?" He told me that "all else must be put aside" and said I "was called of God the Father." The Lord directed me to Psalm 112:1: "Blessed is the man who fears the Lord who finds great delight in His Commands."

The Lord said: "We will start tomorrow," and directed me to Joshua 1: 7, "Be strong and very courageous. Be careful to obey all the law my servant Moses gave you; do not turn from it to the right or to the left, that you may be successful wherever you go."

Then the Lord said to me: *"Do this so we can meet. Prepare to Listen. I will tell you this for the reason I will tell you. I have much to tell you. This will come to you every day. You will take notes every day in a special book."*

"Go to Psalm 24:7,"

> "Lift up your heads, O you gates
> Be lifted up, you ancient doors,
> That the King of glory may come in."

Then Lord then told me to come back to Him in the morning.

Monday, 30th January, 2012, Time: 9:00 a.m.

It is early and I am ready to meet with the Lord. "Father, I come before You and I am prepared to meet with You. I stand in awe of this and I pray that I will fulfil the task that You have set aside for me to do. I am ready and I pray that our time will be private and without any interruptions. I pray for stillness in my heart so that this will be done according to Your will. I undertake to do this and I am willing to do this. My life is in Your hands as I have surrendered to You completely. I pray in Jesus' Mighty Name. Amen."

The Lord said to me:
"Go to Psalm 123,"

"I lift up my eyes to you,
To you whose throne is in heaven.
As the eyes of slaves look to
The hand of their master,
As the eyes of a maid look to
The hand of her mistress,
So our eyes look to the Lord our God
Till he shows us his mercy.
Have mercy on us, O Lord,
Have mercy on us,
For we have endured much contempt.
We have endured much ridicule
From the proud,
Much contempt from the arrogant."

Tuesday, 31 January, 2012, Time: 9:00 a.m.

"This task is for you. So it is with you. You have received much contempt from the proud. Now then those days are over. Never again will you go through that." Yes Lord, thank you. *"I am with you always."* Yes Lord, thank you.

"The arrogance of the world is reaching the heavens and their contempt for Me has reached its fill. I am about to bring My power down from heaven upon this world for all the proud to see."
Yes Lord. *"Now the time of this hour is upon the world."* Yes Lord.
"So then, we will begin." Yes Lord. *"Listen carefully."* Yes Lord.
"All have seen My creation, they know that My creation is real, yet they deny Me. I have given mankind a beautiful creation with such glory and majesty. Fine- tuned in every respect. Yet they deny their Creator. They seek answers for themselves. They create reasons for what they want to believe. They take the swallow and look at its fine feathers and see its flight yet they deny Me. They take the ocean and its wondrous creatures, yet they see Me not. They look to the mountains and they climb them, yet they see Me not. They see the flowers and the wonderful fruit, yet they see Me not. They seek their own answers. They theorize and contemplate—yet they see Me not. Are they blind? No, it is arrogance!

"They wonder not how this came to be. No they deny the creation therefore they deny Me. I am the Creator, I give life. I give the air they breathe and the food they eat. How then do they not see?
They have no excuse! They have no excuse! I have given My life for the arrogant, yet they deny Me and their arrogance stinks to high heaven. It has reached My nostrils. Mankind, the human race, has taken Me for granted. They have spurned My attempts to show them the wonderful scientific mysteries and how it all fits together to work as one. They take all for granted never looking up to the hand that created this. Their arrogance surpasses all understanding! Yes their arrogance! Go to Job 12," "Then Job replied:

'Doubtless you are the people, and wisdom will die with you! But I have a mind as well as you; I am not inferior to you; who does not know all these things? I have become a laughing stock to my friends, though I called upon God and he answered—a mere laughingstock, though righteous and blameless! Men at ease have contempt for misfortune as the fate of those whose feet are slipping.

The tents of marauders are undisturbed, and those who provoke God are secure – those who carry their god in their hands. But ask the animals, and they will teach you or the birds of the air, and they will tell you; or speak to the earth, and it will teach you, or let the fish of the sea inform you. Which of all these does not know that the hand of the Lord has done this? In his hand is the life of every creature and the breath of all mankind. Does not the ear test words as the tongue tastes food? Is not wisdom found among the aged? Does not long life bring understanding? To God belong wisdom and power; counsel and understanding are his. What he tears down cannot be rebuilt; the man he imprisons cannot be released. If he holds back the waters, there is drought; if he lets them loose, they devastate the land.

"'To him belong strength and victory; both deceived and deceiver, are his. He leads counselors away stripped and makes fools of judges. He takes off the shackles put on by kings and ties a loincloth around their waist. He leads priests away stripped and overthrows men long established. He silences the lips of trusted advisers and takes away the discernment of elders. He pours contempt of nobles and disarms the mighty. He reveals the deep things of darkness and brings deep shadows into the light. He makes nations great, and destroys them, he enlarges nations, and disperses them. He deprives the leaders of the earth of their reason; he sends them wandering through a trackless waste. They grope in darkness with no light; He makes them stagger like drunkards.'"

"So now this mere mortal man Job understood the wondrous deeds of his God. Where is his arrogance? He stood for what he could see. He wondered on all this. His reasoning came to a conclusion. What reasoning has mankind come to now? What can he see?

"I will tell you, he sees but he cannot see! No he is blind in his arrogance! Arrogance! Arrogance! Arrogance! His arrogance is his blindness. How then shall I, the Mighty Creator of heaven and earth, see such a thing as this? What do I do with this? How do I reason with man? I can't say 'Come let us reason'. Why can I not? Because man is unable to reason! Why can he not reason? He is blinded by his arrogance! What is arrogance, I ask you, is it not pride? Yes, of course it is—pride!

"What has man got to be proud of? He has been given everything he has. It all comes from creation. Who is the creation? Is it not the Creator? So man, what have you got to say? What is your reason? Do you suppose that in your arrogance and in your pride, you are the Creator? I ask you this now? Are you—Me? No, you are a created being! Can you give life? Can a created being, create? Can you make a tree or a turtle in the sea? Can you? Where were you when I laid the foundations of the earth? Where were you when I separated the waters? Yes, I ask you—where were you?"

The Lord said: *"Go to Job 3,"*

"After this Job opened his mouth and cursed the day of his birth. He said: 'May the day of my birth perish, and the night it was said, "A boy is born!" That day – may it turn to darkness; may God above not care about it; may no light shine upon it. May darkness and deep shadow claim it once more; may a cloud settle over it; may blackness overwhelm its light, that night – may thick darkness seize it; may it not be included among the days of the year nor be entered in any of the months. May that night be barren; may no shout of joy be heard in it. May those who curse days curse that day, those who are ready to rouse Leviathan. May its morning stars become dark; may it wait for daylight in vain and not see the first rays of dawn, For it did not shut the doors of the womb on me to hide trouble from my eyes. Why did I not perish at birth and die as I came from the womb? Why were there knees to receive me and breasts that I might be nursed? For now I would be lying down in peace; I would be asleep and at rest with kings and counselors of the earth, who built for themselves places now lying in ruins, with rulers who had gold, who filled their houses with silver. Or why was I not hidden in the ground like a stillborn child, like an infant who never saw the light of day? There the wicked cease from turmoil, and there the weary are at rest. Captives also enjoy their ease; they no longer hear the slave driver's shout. The small and the great are there, and the slave is freed from his master. Why is light given to those in misery, and life to the bitter of soul, to those who long for death that does not come, who search for it more than for hidden treasure, who are filled with gladness and rejoice when they reach the grave? Why is life given to a man whose way is hidden, whom God has hedged in? For sighing comes to me instead of food; my groans pour out like water. What I feared has come upon me; what I dreaded has happened to me. I have no peace, no quietness; I have no rest, but only turmoil."

The anointing falls heavier on me.

"See I have taken this man Job, to bring to you as an example. He was a man of great substance. He feared the Lord his God with all his heart. Satan came to Me and challenged Me and asked if he could 'sift him.' I gave My permission because I knew that Job would stand the test, even when he suffered such great pain."

"Yes and he did wonder why he was born and why he was suffering but he never stepped away from Me. He held close to Me even when his friends came with their opinions. He remained true to Me. He proved faithful, even when his understanding failed him. So I have to ask you, why did he not become arrogant? I will tell you— because he was not filled with pride. He was humble before his God. He understood that humbleness is not weakness before his God, but strength. In his humbleness he remained strong in his faith. He knew that he was My creation. He saw that creation was the work of My hand. He never had any doubt. Even in his simple,uncomplicated life he saw what was there to be seen. How is it then, that mankind of today cannot see what is around him and is so plainly laid down?"

"I say again, it is arrogance which is pride! In man's arrogance he has stepped into the realm of pride. Pride is his downfall. Do you not know that Satan fell from his place in heaven because of pride? I created him in such beauty and he walked with Me and he spoke with Me until pride overtook him and he thought he was equal to Me. Do you not know that the flood came upon man because of arrogance? They bowed down to Satan and he overcame them."

"Go to Genesis 6,"
The Flood
Verse 5: "The Lord saw how great man's wickedness on the earth had become, and that every inclination of the thoughts of his heart was only evil all the time. The Lord was grieved that he had made man on earth, and his heart was filled with pain. So the Lord said, 'I will wipe mankind, whom I have created, from the face of the earth – men and animals, and creatures that move along the ground, and birds of the air – for I am grieved that I have made them.'"

"Do you see how I dealt with the earth in those days, in the days of Noah. Yes I saved Noah and his family from the destruction, but those of arrogance, I destroyed. Today I have given you this to ponder upon for you have chosen your path of destruction. You do not consider

the things of God at all. You continue in your ways and ignore Me and My creation. But wait there is more:

"Why should I consider you? What is it that makes Me want to? Have you ever wondered why I would or should consider you? Do you suppose that I should consider you? You, who have no regard for Me! Have you wondered about this at any time? Have you taken the time to seek Me? Do you not look up at the stars and see My work or was it just a fleeting moment? When I ask you, will you consider Me? How much more must I give you? You have had My Word, the Bible, in book form for 400 years. Is it an ornament in your house or do you even have one? What excuse will you give Me one day when you stand before Me? What will you say? What excuse will you offer Me? Give it some thought I ask you to do this now. Just what will you say? How well I know the answers; yes I do! But I ask you, what will you say? What excuse will you give Me? In your pride and arrogance, just what will you say?"

"Now My daughter, hear My Words for they are for you. Fear nothing but stand in My Name for I have called you to do this. I am with you, never fear." Yes, Lord.

"Shirley go to 1 Thessalonians 5:16 – 18: "Be joyful always, pray continually, give thanks in all circumstances, for this is God's will for you in Christ Jesus." Yes Lord, thank you.

Wednesday, 1 February, 2012, Time: 9:00 a.m.

"Go into all the nations with this Word and warn My people that I am coming soon. They do not hear as they do not Listen. Give them this warning so that they may prepare themselves for My return. Yes I am coming soon and My church sleeps. This is for them so that they will have no excuse. They must hear My voice for they do not hear My Words." Yes Lord. "So then let us begin."

"Soon comes a time upon this world that will bring such calamity that it will be unbearable to withstand. My prophets have warned you through the words they spoke, even John whom I gave the book of Revelation to, while he was on the Isle of Patmos. This book is much understood yet it is only the wise who understand the sign of the times. My people do not exert themselves to seek Me to reveal the Word to them.

"It is difficult but with wisdom it can be understood. Knowledge of the Bible is all that is needed. My people do not study the Bible. They do not seek out the Word for themselves. Much material is available and with the help of the Holy Spirit much can be understood. It takes a keen heart and study to work on this. It is not an easy undertaking but the signs are all around you. The prophecies are being revealed in your time. Just stay awake like the parable of the ten virgins. Those with oil in their lamps knew the time and those without, slept. This is not the time to sleep. This is the time to stay awake. My Word is given to all."

Sunday, 5 February, 2012, Time: 9:30 a.m.

"Shirley this is for you. You once said that you will follow Me." Yes, Lord. "So then let's do this. Take My hand and come with Me. Do not fear for I am near. I will never leave you nor *forsake you. Stay with Me as I have much to tell you. Do not give up as we can continue."* Yes Lord, thank you. *"Why do you fear when there is nothing to fear. I am with you through this. It will be difficult but do not give up. Hold on and you will see."* Yes Lord, thank you. *"Well then let us begin. Since the beginning I have told you that you will do this."* Yes Lord. *"So then why do you doubt?"* Forgive me Lord. *"You are forgiven."* Thank you, Lord.

"I will lead you." Yes Lord, thank you. *"My hand is upon you."* Yes, Lord. *"My day draws closer and the time is short Shirley."* Yes, Lord. *"I have much to tell you. Please just Listen carefully."* Yes, Lord.

"Soon comes a time of great trouble upon this earth as was never before. My people sleep just as the world sleeps. They cannot read the times of change. They see nothing." Yes Lord. *"It is for this reason you have been given this task. You see the times of change."* Yes, Lord I do. *"Yet My people sleep. So then, I ask you to do this for Me."* Yes Lord. *"Tell the world to wake up and to Listen to what I am saying."* Yes Lord. *"They bind up their minds and allow the god of this world to keep it bound. They are blinded by his power."* Yes Lord. *"Let them see this Word for it is I the Lord God Almighty speaking to them. Will they Listen?"* I don't know Lord. *"Well the time is short and I want to warn My people."* Yes Lord, the choice is theirs—they have a free will Lord.

"I am holding you to this now Shirley. We will complete this warning to the world for it is time." Yes, it is late Lord. *"Yes time is short and the world is in the hands of Satan. But I have this Word for them. Let them break free from the power of the enemy and hear My voice for I am speaking to them."* Yes Lord.

"Go to Jeremiah 21:8:

"Furthermore, tell the people, this is what the Lord says: I am setting before you the way of life and the way of death."

Time: 7:35 p.m.

"I have begun to bring this to the people who will Listen." Yes, Lord. *"Let Me tell you this. They are deaf and do not hear!"* Yes Lord. *"So then write down all I tell you. But hold on and continue with Me."* Yes, Lord I will. *"When the anointing lifts, then it is done."* Yes Lord, thank you Lord.

"Go to Romans 9: 27 & 28,

"Isaiah cries out concerning Israel: 'Though the number of the Israelites be like the sand by the sea, only a remnant will be saved. For the Lord will carry out his sentence on earth with speed and finality.'"

"How many will Listen? Yes I come soon! I will begin with a major shock for the world. They will not see it coming. It will be a shock. It will begin with a sound of the trumpet and the earth will shake. The land will tremble and the sea will toss. Men will stand and look and say 'What is this that has come upon the earth?' They will look to the heavens shouting 'What is this?'"

"Shirley, just Listen, wait and Listen." Yes, Lord.

"Come now and let us reason together. Do you want to reason? Then we can reason, says the Lord God Almighty. For if you will lend your ear and Listen to My voice then we can reason. I will tell you of things to come. But if you remain arrogant then you will remain deaf. For what can the deaf hear? They Listen but cannot hear. Go to Psalm 33:4 – 19,"

"For the Word of the Lord is right and true; He is faithful in all he does. The Lord loves righteousness and justice, the earth is full of his unfailing love. By the Word of the Lord were the heavens made, their starry host by the breath of his mouth. He gathers the waters of the sea into jars, he puts the deep into storehouses. Let all the earth fear the Lord; let all the people of the world revere him.

For he spoke, and it came to be; He commanded, and it stood firm. The Lord foils the plans of the nations; He thwarts the purposes of the peoples. But the plans of the Lord stand firm forever, the purposes of his heart through all generations. Blessed is the nation whose God is the Lord, the people he chose for his inheritance.

From heaven the Lord looks down and sees all mankind. From his dwelling place He watches all who live on earth—He who forms the hearts of all, who considers everything they do. No king is saved by the size of his army; no warrior escapes by his great strength. A horse is a vain hope for deliverance; despite all its great strength it cannot save. But the eyes of the Lord are on those who fear him, on those whose hope is in his unfailing love, to deliver them from death and keep them alive in famine.

Monday, 6 February, 2012, Time: 10:03 a.m.

"Shirley this is for you. Go to Psalm 23." Thank you Lord.
"As we go down further into this message you will begin to fear, that is why I gave you Psalm 23." Yes Lord. *"Know that I am with you."* Yes Lord. *"So then let us begin. Listen carefully."* Yes Lord. *"All will stand in awe of you. They will know that you have been called to do this."* Yes Lord. *"Yet some will question this."* Yes Lord. *"Do not Listen to them."* Yes Lord. *"They may question but they will know it is Me, the Lord God Almighty."* Yes Lord. *"You have felt the contempt of many."* Yes Lord. *"You have been called names."* Yes Lord. *"Well then, you have been prepared for this."* Yes Lord.

The Lord directed me to Jeremiah 1:18:

"Today I have made you a fortified city, an iron pillar and a bronze wall to stand against the whole land—against the kings of Judah, its officials, its priests and the people of the land."

"Shirley I have told you that the day will come when you will speak My Words." Yes Lord you did. *"I told you that I would speak through you."* Yes Lord, many years ago. *"Well this is the time."* Yes Lord I am ready. *"So then, you have been told and you have been prepared."* Yes Lord. *"You have suffered contempt have you not?"* Yes Lord. *"You are ready."* Yes Lord. *"Go to Psalm 2:*

"Why do the nations conspire and the peoples plot in vain? The kings of the earth take their stand and the rulers gather together against the Lord and against his Anointed One, 'Let us break their chains,' they say, 'and throw off their fetters.' The One enthroned in heaven laughs, the Lord scoffs at them. Then he rebukes them in his anger and terrifies them in his wrath, saying, 'I have installed my King on Zion, my holy hill.' I will proclaim the decree of the Lord: He said to me, 'You are my Son, today I have become your Father. Ask of me, and I will make the nations your inheritance, the ends of the earth your possession. You will rule them with an iron scepter; You will dash them to pieces like pottery.' Therefore, you kings, be wise; be warned, you rulers of the earth. Serve the Lord with fear and rejoice with trembling, kiss the Son, lest he be angry and you be destroyed in your way, for his wrath can flare up in a moment.

Blessed are all who take refuge in him."

"Now go to Revelation 1:18, "I am the Living One; I was dead, and behold I am alive for ever and ever! And I hold the keys of death and Hades."

"It is to you the people of this earth that I speak to. Yes, I am alive. Do you understand? Do you believe that I am alive? Yes I am alive! This is what I am telling you. I am alive! I came and died for you! I took the sins of the world and My blood was poured out for you. I hung on the tree for you."

"Now go to Revelation 3:20: "Here I am! I stand at the door and knock. If anyone hears my voice and opens the door, I will come in and eat with him, and he with me."

"Do you know that I knock on your door all the time? I call out to you continually. But you are deaf. You cannot hear because of your arrogance, yes your arrogance! Do you know that I hold the keys of Hades? The keys of life and death! But of course in arrogance, you choose death." How sad, Lord. *"Yes My child arrogance is death. But I tell you this, they are blinded by the devil."* Yes Lord, James 4: 7 says, "Submit to God then resist the devil and he will flee." *"Yes but their arrogance stands in their way. How can they submit when they are filled with pride? You see Shirley it is pride that keeps them from Me. They are too great in their own eyes to see Me."* Yes Lord it is sad.

"For generation upon generation I have sent My prophets and teachers into the world and do you know what?" No Lord. *"It is and has always been the humble that seek Me. Yes sometimes I have to intervene and I try to do this but even then the arrogant remain proud."* Yes Lord. Then the Lord showed me a chess board. Lord what is this for?

"This is how I try to move in their lives. I move the knight to defend them. I put the pawns in their way to direct them but they cannot see that they are stumped. They never ask Me for direction. Some move ahead anyway and others stay put. Either way it is a hard and difficult road. But they never seek Me for direction. No they play the game of life all on their own. You see, to many, life is just a game. They do not realize that life is a choice, yes it either leads to life or to death and many choose death because of pride. You see Satan chose death through his pride and now his children choose death because of pride."

I thought to myself, the Lord really hates pride. *"Yes, Shirley because pride, is death.*

It is the downfall of man. Disobedience and arrogance result in pride. Adam and Eve led by example.Disobedience led to arrogance, they wanted to know both evil and good. Yes so pride overtook them like Satan and they were cast out of the garden just as Satan was cast out of heaven." Yes I can see Lord that pride is a fatal error. *"Yes, Shirley, even in their normal lives. It costs them dearly in their marriages, home life, and in every aspect of their day to day lives. Arrogance leads to death."*

Tuesday, 7 February, 2012, Time: 9:45 a.m.

"Listen carefully as we continue." Yes Lord.
"Shirley the time has come for the people of the world to hear My voice." Yes Lord, it is time because they are children of darkness. *"Yes, Shirley they live in the night and do not see the light of the Kingdom of God. Shirley, write this down, word for word."* Yes Lord. *"All of the world lives in perpetual darkness. It is only the lights among them that shine like bright stars before Me. These are those who are Mine. Each one of My children, shine as bright lights in this dark world. It is for them that I have given the world time. It is for them, that I will come, for they are Mine. My children belong to Me. These are those who have suffered persecution for their faith. They are scoffed at by those who live in darkness. The children of the dark are blind like bats. They go about their lives living in the dark. But My children know Me and they speak to Me. These are the ones I love because they love Me. They see Me as their God and My children obey Me. They seek Me with their whole heart and they live to obey Me. These are My children."*

Yes, Lord, but there are some people who proclaim Jesus, yet lead their own lives contrary to the Scriptures.

"Yes and it is to these children that I speak to now. Let them see how they live. Is it for Me or do they live for themselves and for what it is, they want? Do they come to Me and ask Me, what I want for them? You see Shirley many call only for their pleasures. Yes I hear them but do they live for Me? You see to love Me is to obey Me." Lord, many live with one foot in the light and one foot in the dark. They are lukewarm Lord? *"Yes and they must know and hear these Words for they are the ones I will spew out of My mouth and say to them, away with you, I do not know you. To love Me is to obey Me. My sheep hear My voice because they are My children and they live in the light. Then there are many that proclaim My Name but do not know My voice. These are like the five virgins that did not have oil in their lamps. They did not hear My call as the other five virgins did and went out to meet Me. Shirley the time is short and I come soon to take what is Mine."* Yes Lord. *"Are My people ready? Are their lamps full? They do not make time to meet with their Lord even to just speak a few words to Me each day. I wait to hear from them but they do not come to Me."* Yes, Lord life is hectic and exhausting. *"All I ask is for them to know My voice. They need to know My voice, to know Me? I speak to them through My Word. I died on the cross for them. I hung on the tree for them. All I ask is for them to come each day and in prayer and petition and to do this is to obey Me. To obey Me is to love Me. I love them so much that I died for them."* Yes Lord. I cannot think, I am so upset, I can only say, yes, Lord.

"Do you know that some come to Me only when they are in trouble. I never hear from them, only when their lives are in a mess. Then only do they come and ask for help. If they had come to Me in prayer and if they know My voice, they would be in My perfect will for their lives. They would have direction and would move in faith. Is it too much to ask from My people? Come to Me in prayer and come to hear My voice Seek your Savior; you made Me Lord of your life. Your life became Mine and you were cleansed of all sin, forgiven and washed by My blood. I said, come to the Father in My Name and I will do it. I tell you the

truth, unless you repent and return to Me with all your heart you will not hear My voice and your lamp will be empty. My sheep know My voice. I am your Shepherd! Go to Matthew 5:14 – 16:

"You are the light of the world. A city on a hill cannot be hidden. Neither do people light a lamp and put it under a bowl. Instead they put it on its stand, and it gives light to everyone in the house. In the same way, let your light shine before men that they may see your good deeds and praise your Father in heaven."

"My people must be the light in this dark world. Let your light shine brightly!"

Wednesday, Thursday 8 & 9February, 2012

Received personal word.

Friday, 10 February, 2012, Time: 9:56 a.m.

"Yes My child let's begin. I have given you this task to do." Yes, Lord. *"Therefore, I will be with you until it is done."* Thank you, Lord. *"We will work together to do this."* Yes, Lord. *"The day has dawned upon this earth for all My Word to begin to be fulfilled. The Word I have given My prophets will be done as it has been written.*

The world stands aloof to My Word but in a moment it will be upon them. So then, this is the reason for this warning. The day is near and nothing will stop My Words from being fulfilled; it is written therefore it will be." Yes, Lord.

"Now My child this is for you. All who read My Words will know that it is I speaking to you. They will see My hand is upon you." Yes Lord. *"I have chosen you before you were born to do this. I have been with you and carried you through all that has come upon you in your life. Many times you have been brought under by those who have deceived you."* Yes Lord. *"So then, know that I will not allow anyone to destroy what I have given you to do."* Yes Lord. (I realized that the Lord is determined to complete this task and will not stand by and allow anyone to stop this. I also realized that He wants me to understand this). Lord, I understand.

"Shirley the beginning of the end according to My written Word is soon to be fulfilled." Yes Lord. *"This is why I am giving this warning. I am the Alpha and the Omega, the Beginning and the End. I am the Righteous Judge. Shirley you have had a difficult life. You have attempted many things and it always seems to go nowhere. You have success but never reach the place you set out to reach."* Yes Lord. *"Why do you think this happened to you?"* Lord, I never understood.

"Well I am going to tell you now. It was Me. I let you go ahead and do what was in your heart but I held back the rewards." Yes Lord, I seemed to try and never completely succeed and reach my ultimate goals. *"These were all tests you went through. I tried your patience and your perseverance. I tested your faith. You must understand that I needed to test you."* Yes Lord, I understand. *"Shirley there were times when you buckled under the strain but you always came back to Me and wanted to start again. You would pick up the pieces and go forward. You wanted to run away at times."* Yes Lord. *"You came against many solid walls, not knowing which way to go."* Yes Lord. I could not turn left or right and the road ahead was closed to me. I did not want to go back so I would just sit and wait for things to change. *"Yes Shirley, this is patience and perseverance."* Yes Lord. I learned to just take one day at a time and wait upon You. I learned that Your timing is perfect and that when doors closed around me, it meant that I had to wait until a door opened. Sometimes more than one door would open and I was not sure which door to enter. So I would wait on You until I knew which door to enter. Lord I knew that if I entered the wrong door it would cause some harm and would waste precious time. So I just waited on direction from You Lord.

"Shirley so you agree that you stood in faith." Yes Lord when there is nothing I can do then I wait on You. I always try and do what I can in my capacity as a human on earth and when I can't change or move a situation, I hand it over to You and lay my life at Your feet and then wait on You. *"So I ask you, is this faith?"* Yes Lord, it is faith. *"So faith is what has driven you?"* Yes Lord. *"Shirley do you see how tests and trials in life teach patience and perseverance?"* "Those who wait upon the Lord will never be put to shame," came to my mind. *"Yes Shirley."* I have learned that the Lord's timing is always perfect. Many times I have seen this in my life and in the lives of others.

"Shirley I needed you to learn this lesson in life as I do all My children. I know that this will help many to understand. Faith becomes stronger with each test and trial." Yes Lord, I realize that each trial is a test and is learned through patience, perseverance and faith. *"Go to Psalm 46.1 – 5,*

"God is our Refuge and Strength,
An ever-present help in trouble.
Therefore we will not fear,
Though the earth gives way
And the mountains fall into
The heart of the sea,
Though its waters roar and foam
And the mountains quake with their surging.
There is a river whose streams
Make glad the city of God,
The holy place where the Most High dwells.
God is within her, she will not fall;
God will help her at break of day."

"Shirley you were brought to this place to understand faith. Yes you must have faith and believe in Me but you also must have faith in life that comes with trials and tribulations. You see if you have faith and stand in faith, all things are possible even when circumstances don't make any sense at the time. Many times things happen and a reason for it cannot be found, just know that I am working in you. Satan gets the blame and yes he deserves it mostly, but there are times when I step into your life to bring change to it."

Yes, Lord. *"You see without faith you cannot please God."* Yes Lord, I know that over the years I have learned to persevere with patience and to wait on You.

Saturday, 11 February, 2012, Time: 9:30 a.m.

"Shirley, please Listen carefully." Yes Lord. *"I have taken you into the issue of faith. So it is with all My children. They must stand in faith. This is the birth of Christianity. Without faith they cannot please Me. They must learn to stand in faith! The time that the world is entering into will require faith. The hearts of men will be tested as never before. Without faith they will fall."* Yes Lord.

"Each one must learn to stand and stand in faith. Their hearts must be open to receive. Their lamps must be full of oil. They must not sleep but stay awake and watch for the time of great trial is here. The world as you know it will change. Evil will prevail as never before. I speak to My children and I say to you, draw close to Me for 'now is the time.' Shirley." Yes Lord. *"I have much to tell you to write down."* Yes Lord. *"I am giving you this to bring warning to My people. Now is the time! The time foretold in the Bible is coming about soon. Many prophecies are being fulfilled as this is written. The world is heading for its climax and the new awaits it. I am coming soon and I say to you all, this is a true and faithful Word, I am coming soon! I want you all to understand this and I ask you all to prepare for Me. You see unless you are ready for Me, you will not see Me. I come for those who have oil in their lamps. Shirley, go to Matthew 11:12 & 13:* (Jesus speaking)

"From the days of John the Baptist until now, the Kingdom of heaven has been forcefully advancing and forceful men lay hold of it. For all the prophets and the law prophesied until John."

Time: 1:00 p.m.

"The time has begun and the day has arrived for this to be given to those who will Listen. I have done this so that those who will Listen will hear My voice. Mighty men of ages gone have spoken about these events that are happening now.
It is up to each and every one who reads and hears My voice to Listen. The dawn has broken and the time is at hand. Yes, My time is not your time, but the time I speak of here, is time that involves both you and I. This time is at hand. Shirley, go to Isaiah 12: "Songs of Praise : In that day you will say;

'I will praise you, O Lord
Although you were angry with me,
Your anger has turned away
And you have comforted me.
Surely God is my salvation;
I will trust and not be afraid.
The Lord, the Lord,
Is my strength and my song;
He has become my salvation.
With joy you will draw water
From the wells of salvation.
In that day you will say;
"Give thanks to the Lord,
Call on his Name,
Make known among the nations
What he has done,
And proclaim that his Name is exalted.
Sing to the Lord, for he has
Done glorious things;
Let this be known to all the world.
Shout aloud and sing for joy, people of Zion,
For great is the Holy One of Israel among you."

"Now Listen carefully. Go to Isaiah 24:

The Lord's Devastation of the Earth.

"See, the Lord is going to lay waste the earth
And devastate it;
He will ruin its face and
Scatter its inhabitants –
It will be the same
For priest as for people,
For master as for servant,

For mistress as for maid, For seller as for buyer,
For borrower as for lender,
For debtor as for creditor,
The earth will be completely laid waste and totally plundered.
The Lord has spoken this word.
The earth dries up and withers,
The world languishes and withers,
The exalted of the earth languish.
The earth is defiled by its people;
They have disobeyed the laws,
Violated the statutes
And broken the everlasting covenant.
Therefore a curse consumes the earth;
Its people must bear their guilt.
Therefore earth's inhabitants are burned up,
And very few are left,
The new wine dries up and the vine withers,
All the merrymakers groan.
The gaiety of the tambourines is stilled,
The noise of the revelers has stopped,
The joyful harp is silent.
No longer do they drink wine with a song;
The beer is bitter to its drinkers.
The ruined city lies desolate;
The entrance to every house is barred.
In the streets they cry out for wine;
All joy turns to gloom,
All gaiety is banished from the earth.
The city is left in ruins, its gate is battered to pieces.
So it will be on earth
And among the nations,
As when an olive tree is beaten,
Or as when gleanings are left after the grape harvest.
They raise their voices, they shout for joy,
From the west they acclaim the Lord's majesty.
Therefore in the east give glory to the Lord;
Exalt the name of the Lord, the God of Israel,
In the islands of the sea.
From the ends of the earth we hear singing:
'Glory to the Righteous One.'
But I said, 'I waste away, I waste away!
Woe to me!The treacherous betray!
With treachery the treacherous betray!'
Terror and pit and snare await you,
O people of the earth.
Whoever flees at the sound of terror
Will fall into a pit;
Whoever climbs out of the pit will be caught in a snare.
The floodgates of the heavens are opened,
The foundations of the earth shake. The earth is broken up,

The earth is split asunder, the earth is thoroughly shaken.
The earth reels like a drunkard.
It sways like a hut in the wind;
So heavy upon it is the guilt of its rebellion that it falls –
Never to rise again.
In that day the Lord will punish
The powers in the heavens above
And the kings on the earth below.
They will be herded together like prisoners bound in a dungeon;
They will be shut up in prison and be punished after many days.
The moon will be abashed, the sun ashamed;
For the Lord Almighty will reign
On Mount Zion and in Jerusalem, and before its elders gloriously."

"Shirley I want you to Listen carefully to these next Words." Yes Lord. *"Take off your pride, you people. Cast it aside for the day is near. I come with vengeance soon and it will not be nice. It will be disaster upon disaster. There will be: No escape, No place to hide and No place to run to. Yes cast aside your pride. Your arrogance is death. Listen will you? What the Lord God Almighty, Creator of Heaven and Earth says to you today. The God of the Universe speaks to you today. Will you hear?"*

Sunday, 12 February, 2012, Time: 10:08 a.m.

"Shirley this is what I say to the people of this world. Stand ready to receive what the Lord God Almighty has ready to pour out upon this world. I have seen all. Nothing is hidden from Me. I know your plans and your schemes but I tell you the truth, you will receive all that you have done. You stand ready to devour My people with a sword in your hand. You stand ready to shut them up. But it is I the Lord Almighty that has seen this. You hide your schemes in your pockets—the plans of the destruction of My people. Yes I have seen all. You cannot stand to hear their words, can you? It hurts your ears. Yes in your arrogance, it pains you. But you see you cannot shut them up because the Word is written and what is written will be. No one on earth can change that. It will be done as it is written." The anointing falls heavier on me and the Lord says to me.

"Shirley it pains Me to say these Words to this world but the truth stands firm." Yes Lord. *"I can tell you this; nothing will stop what is coming."* Yes Lord. The thought came to me about Jonah. He had success in ministering the Word of warning from God to the town of Nineveh—they repented and turned to God. The Lord heard my mind and he answered saying to me… *"It is done Shirley, the Word will be fulfilled as it is. Nothing can stop this."* Yes Lord. *It has begun, the world is racing towards its destiny. Go to Matthew 24:6 -9:* (Jesus speaking to his disciples)

"You will hear of wars and rumors of wars, but see to it that you are not alarmed. Such things must happen, but the end is still to come. Nation will rise against nation, and kingdom against kingdom. There will be famines and earthquakes in various places. All these are the beginning of birth pains. Then you will be handed over to be persecuted and put to death, and you will be hated by all the nations because of me."

The thought came to me that all this is happening now. Christians are being persecuted in many countries and churches are being destroyed. There are uprisings in some countries and people are fighting their own governments; famine in other countries and even the smaller earthquakes do not make headlines any longer. So the birth pains have begun. I then had this thought—I have given natural birth to three children so I understand birth pains. They start off gradually and can continue for some time until the pains get worse and more frequent. Then they come, one upon another until the baby is born and the last pains are the worst. So if the beginning of birth pains is less painful than the final pains, we have only tasted the beginning of the birth pains for what is soon coming.

"Shirley your thoughts are correct. The world has some time to go but as time passes the birth pains will grow stronger." Yes Lord and after the baby is born, joy fills the mother's heart and the pain is gone. *"Yes Shirley and so it will be on earth."* Yes Lord. *"Shirley all I am giving you is for the world, those who will Listen."* Lord. *"So it will be."* Yes Lord. *"Stay close to me until I give you all you need to do this. It is something that is going to take time."* Yes, Lord I can see. *" So then, come as often as you can."* Yes, Lord.

Monday, 13 February, 2012, Time: 9:20 a.m.

"I want you to wait until I give you the Word." Yes Lord.
"I have given you this Word because My return is imminent."
The anointing falls heavier on me again and I wait on the Lord. *"Shirley I want you to go to Revelation 3: 20:*

"Here I am! I stand at the door and knock. If anyone hears my voice and opens the door, I will come in and eat with him and him with me."

"This is My call to all those who will Listen to My Words. My heart is open to all who will come to Me for now is the time. I say to you 'come' for the time is now. I am beginning with My final arrangements to return to take those who are mine."

Please, I ask you in the Name of Jesus to listen to what the Lord is saying to you.

"People of earth, I am bringing this Word to My daughter for you. I am calling you to come to Me for the time is now. Do you know that Noah took many years to build the Ark and in all those years he was ridiculed and scoffed at. People stood and watched him build the Ark and never saw the time that was coming.

"Their destruction waited patiently until the time came and then there was nowhere to run. This warning is for you—you who will Listen. All that is coming will happen suddenly and there will be nowhere to hide, just as in the days of Noah. I do nothing until I reveal it to My prophets. This is for those who will hear. The day will come upon you suddenly and without notice and you will try to hide but there will be no place to hide. Go to Revelation 3: 19:

"Those whom I love I rebuke and discipline,
so be earnest and repent."

"This is My call to all those who claim to be Christians and yet do not know Me. This is My call to all those who have never known Me; I say to you all, come now is the time. It is late, some will be first and some will be last, but My call is, come now! Go to Matthew 6:5-15: (Jesus speaking)

"And when you pray, do not be like the hypocrites, for they love to pray standing in the synagogues and on the street corners to be seen by men. I tell you the truth, they have received their reward in full.

But when you pray, go into your room, close the door and pray to your Father, who is unseen. Then your Father, who sees what is done in secret, will reward you. And when you pray, do not keep on babbling like pagans, for they think they will be heard because of their many words. Do not be like them, for your Father knows what you need before you ask him. This is how you should pray: Our father in heaven, hallowed be your name, Your kingdom come, Your will be done on earth as it is in heaven. Give us today our daily bread, forgive us our debts, As we also have forgiven our debtors. And lead us not into temptation, but deliver us from the evil one. For if you forgive men when they sin against you, your heavenly Father will also forgive you. But if you do not forgive men their sins, your Father will not forgive your sins."

"Shirley, the time is now. People must repent and serve their God with a pure heart and with clean hands. Their God is not fooled and knows the hearts of men. I say to you all, the Father looks down from heaven and searches the hearts, for those who seek Him. Now is the time to pray. Now is the time to repent. Do not allow your pride to steal what is given to you. Come now is the time! Shirley, the world stands ready for judgment. It is ripe for judgment." Yes Lord, time is running out.

"Go to Psalm 14,"

"The fool says in his heart, 'There is no God,' They are corrupt, their deeds are vile; there is no one who does good. The Lord looks down from heaven on the sons of men to see if there are any who understand, any who seek God. All have turned aside, they have together become corrupt, there is no one who does good, not even one. Will evildoers never learn – those who devour my people as men eat bread and who do not call on the Lord? There they are, overwhelmed with dread, for God is present in the company of the righteous. You evildoers frustrate the plans of the poor, but the Lord is their refuge. Oh, that salvation for Israel would come out of Zion!
When the Lord restores the fortunes of his people, let Jacob rejoice and Israel be glad!"

Oh Lord, if only they will Listen. My heart is sore as I think of those I know who will not hear. *"Yes Shirley, they are foolish but I will never stop calling them."* Yes Lord.

Wednesday, 15 February, 2012,Time: 9: 00 a.m.

"I have seen your heart and you are ready and eager to do this." Yes Lord. *"So then, we will continue. It pleases Me to know that you have My concerns upon your heart."* Yes Lord you are my Lord and You are calling out to people to Listen and take notice that our world has

changed and is heading in a different direction. Things are not the same, the world is changing Lord. *"Yes Shirley, things that are happening now are setting the path the world will travel on. It is paving its way to its conclusion."* Yes Lord.

"Be careful to write what I say." Yes Lord. *"To those who will Listen and turn to Me, I will receive. But to those who will not Listen, I will not receive. They will be cast into the depths of hell where weeping and gnashing of teeth never end. Yes, you see all things have a beginning and an ending. The beginning has gone and the end is near. All life has a beginning and an end. All things begin and all things end. I am the Alpha and the Omega, the Beginning and the End. So if I am the end, then that is the end. Let those who will hear, Listen to what I am saying. I have done all there is to be done. I came and I died and I rose again. My blood was given to you so that you can be saved. It is by My blood that your sins are forgiven. I am that I am! Go to Matthew 3:16 & 17:*

"As soon as Jesus was baptized, he went up out of the water. At that moment heaven opened, and he saw the Spirit of God descending like a dove and lighting on him. And a voice from heaven said, 'This is my Son, whom I love; with him I am well pleased.'"

Lord, this shows the Father, the Holy Spirit and the Son. *"Yes Shirley, all authority in heaven and on earth is Mine. I hold it all. I have been given the keys and I hold the power in My hand. If you deny Me on earth, My Father will deny you in heaven."* Lord, I pray that this Word will touch hearts and they will change. *"Shirley many live in such arrogance that they cannot see and cannot hear."* Yes Lord I have met people like that. When Your Name comes up in conversation they get up and leave. The god of this age has blinded them. *"Yes Shirley, they live in darkness and the light blinds them; that is why they walk away. Shirley I will never stop calling them. I put My labourers across their paths. I came for all and I will continue to call while there is still time. My people must pray for the lost so that they may be found."* Yes, Lord.
"Go to Luke 24:1 – 8: The Resurrection.

"On the first day of the week, very early in the morning, the women took the spices they had prepared and went to the tomb. They found the stone rolled away from the tomb, but when they entered, they did not find the body of the Lord Jesus. While they were wondering about this, suddenly two men in clothes that gleamed like lightning stood beside them. In their fright the women bowed down with their faces to the ground, but the men said to them, 'Why do you look for the living among the dead? He is not here; He has risen! Remember how he told you, while he was still with you in Galilee:

"The Son of Man must be delivered into the hands of sinful men, be crucified and on the third day be raised again.'" Then they remembered his words."

"Shirley, I came knowing I would be crucified and I willingly gave My life for all." Yes Lord You did. *"How much more would I not warn My people that I come again?"* Yes Lord it is written in the Bible that You will come again, just as it is written that You would be born on earth. *"So it will be Shirley. The day and the hour are unknown. That is why it is important to call to people to Listen to what I am saying. The signs of the times have begun."*

I recalled Matthew 24:36 in my mind—"No one knows about that day or hour, not even the angels in heaven, nor the Son, but only the Father." The Lord heard my mind. *"Yes, Shirley no one will know.*

Go to Matthew 24:42: (Jesus speaking)

"Therefore keep watch, because you do not know on
what day your Lord will come."

*"I will come like a thief in the night, so I say to you keep watch and be ready for you know
not the day or the hour. Go to Matthew 25:1 – 13:* The Ten Virgins. Jesus speaking,

"At that time the kingdom of heaven will be like ten virgins who took their lamps and went
out to meet the bridegroom. Five of them were foolish and five were wise. The foolish ones
took their lamps but did not take any oil with them. The wise, however, took oil in jars along
with their lamps. The bridegroom was a long time in coming, and they all became drowsy
and fell asleep. At midnight the cry rang out: 'Here's the bridegroom! come out to meet him!'
Then all the virgins woke up and trimmed their lamps. The foolish ones said to the wise,
'Give us some oil; our lamps are going out.'
'No,' they replied, 'there may not be enough for both us and you.' Instead, go to those who
sell oil and buy some for yourselves. But while they were on their way to buy the oil, the
bridegroom arrived. The virgins who were ready went with him to the wedding banquet. And
the door was shut. Later the others also came, 'Sir! Sir!' they said. 'Open the door for us!'
But he replied, 'I tell you the truth, I don't know you.' Therefore keep watch, because you do
not know the day or the hour."

Lord you have been saying that we must keep our lamps full of oil. *"Yes Shirley just as all
must keep watch. Wait and watch for I come soon. This is the Word to all who claim they
know Me. Take this as a warning and keep it in your heart for once the door shuts, it is
closed. Take care to come to know Me. My sheep know My voice. Come let us dine together
that we may talk. Come now, for now is the time. For those who do not know Me, I invite you
to open the door to your heart and invite Me in, that we may dine together."*

Thursday, 16 February, 2012, Time: 1:37 p.m.

"Shirley, write this down carefully." Yes, Lord. *"I have begun this work with you to warn the
peoples of earth to heed what I say to them. They must Listen and hear what I speak to them
for the world is heading for tumultuous times. Many lives will be lost for the day of reckoning
is here. The road is narrow and few find it. I call on all those who have entered the gate to
the narrow road and I say this to them; if you love Me you will obey Me. You will love the
Lord your God with all your heart, mind and soul. You will love your neighbor as you love
yourself. You will submit to your master in obedience to Me. You will honor Me and love Me
as I love and honor you. You will be good parents to those children I have blessed you with
and the children will honor you. Do to others as you will have them do unto you. Give to the
poor for you will be blessed. Take care of your parents for they raised you. Love your wife as
you love me. Wives, love your husbands as they submit to Me. Marriage is sacred and must
be honored. Family life is from the Father. He has given you family. Love your family and
stand together. Yes love one another. Love conquers all. Shirley, go to Matthew 16:24 – 28:*
(Jesus speaking)

"Then Jesus said to his disciples: 'If anyone would come after me, he must deny himself and take up his cross and follow me. For whoever wants to save his life will lose it, but whoever loses his life for me will find it. What good will it be for a man if he gains the whole world, yet forfeits his soul? Or what can a man give in exchange for his soul? For the Son of Man is going to come in his Father's glory with his angels, and then he will reward each person according to what he has done. I tell you the truth, some who are standing here will not taste death before they see the Son of Man coming in his Kingdom.'"

"Since I spoke those Words until now, the same call is reaching out to you today. Will you hear these Words, will you? I say again, My sheep know My voice. Call out to Me and I will hear you."

Lord that is so beautiful. *"Yes Shirley, I stand at the door of many hearts waiting to come in."* Please, people hear the Word of the Lord while there still is time.

"The road is narrow and I say to those who do not know Me 'come.' Find the narrow road and get off the road that leads to hell. It is wide and filling up to capacity, come to Me like little children, come now." The Lord is calling the people of this world. Please Listen to his call.
"Since the beginning of time I have waited for this moment. To come and take those who are Mine. I come soon, sooner than you think. Pick up your cross and follow Me. Go to Matthew 28:18 & 20:

"Then Jesus came to them and said; 'All authority in heaven and on earth has been given to me…and surely I am with you always, to the very end of the age.'"

"You see My Word is the same Yesterday, today and forever. Shirley, go to Luke 15:3 – 7:
"Then Jesus told them this parable; 'Suppose one of you has a hundred sheep and loses one of them. Does he not leave the ninety-nine in the open country and go after the lost sheep until he finds it? And when he finds it, he joyfully puts it on his shoulders and goes home. Then he calls his friends and neighbors together and says, "Rejoice with me; I have found my lost sheep," I tell you that in the same way there will be more rejoicing in heaven over one sinner who repents than over ninety-nine righteous persons who do not need to repent.'"

"Shirley the truth is that with each sinner that repents, heaven sings and rejoices. My love for the people on earth is unmeasured and I want not one to perish." Yes Lord. *"I call out to those who will hear My voice today and say to each one; repent and come to Me that there may be great rejoicing in heaven. This is My call; repent for now is the time of grace. Mercy abounds and waits on you, come now!"*

Friday, 17 February, 2012, Time: 8:31a.m.

"Shirley." Yes, Lord. *"Let us begin. I have begun this in your life so that you can stand as a witness to what I am saying to this world."* Yes Lord. *"Will you stand as Witness?"* Yes Lord. *"Do not fear as I speak through you."* Yes Lord. *"Go to Psalm 66—this is for you."*

"Shout with joy to God, all the earth! Sing the glory of his name; make his praise glorious! Say to God, 'How awesome are your deeds! So great is your power that your enemies cringe before you. All the earth bows down to you; They sing praise to you, they sing praise to your name.' Come and see what God has done, how awesome his works in man's behalf! He turned the sea into dry land, they passed through the waters on foot—come, let us rejoice in him. He rules forever by his power, his eyes watch the nations— let not the rebellious rise up against him. Praise our God, O peoples, let the sound of his praise be heard; He has preserved our lives and kept our feet from slipping. For you, O God, tested us; you refined us like silver. You brought us into prison and laid burdens on our backs. You let men ride over our heads; we went through fire and water, but you brought us to a place of abundance. I will come to your temple with burnt offerings and fulfill my vows to you – vows my lips promised and my mouth spoke when I was in trouble. I will sacrifice fat animals to you and an offering of rams; I will offer bulls and goats. Come and Listen, all you who fear God; let me tell you what he has done for me. I cried out to him with my mouth; His praise was on my tongue. If I cherished sin in my heart, the Lord would not have listened, but God has surely listened and heard my voice in prayer. Praise be to God, who has not rejected my prayer or withheld his love from me!"

Thank you Lord, Yes, I will fulfil the vow I made to You and be Your witness.

"Go to John 14:1 – 4: (Jesus speaking)

"Do not let your hearts be troubled. Trust in God; trust also in Me. In My Father's house are many rooms; if it were not so, I would have told you. I am going there to prepare a place for you. And if I go and prepare a place for you, I will come back and take you to be with Me that you also may be where I am. You know the way to the place where I am going."

"Shirley, this is what I am saying to My people today; I am ready for you. All is prepared. Are you ready for Me? I come soon, sooner than many believe. Shirley, the time is now! My people must prepare and be ready. I am ready for them so they must be ready for Me." Yes Lord. *"I am in the Father and My Father is in Me and I wait upon My Father just as you wait upon Me. Go to Romans 5:15 – 21:*

"But the gift is not like the trespass. For if the many died by the trespass of the one man, how much more did God's grace and the gift that came by the grace of the one man, Jesus Christ, overflow to the many! Again, the gift of God is not like the result of the one man's sin: the judgment followed one sin and brought condemnation, but the gift followed many trespasses and brought justification. For if, by the trespass of the one man, death reigned through that one man, how much more will those who receive God's abundant provision of grace and the gift of righteousness reign in life through one man, Jesus Christ. Consequently, just as the result of one trespass was condemnation for all men, so also the result of one act of righteousness was justification that brings life for all men. For just as through the disobedience of the one man the many were made sinners, so also through the obedience of the one man the many will be made righteous. The law was added so that the trespass might increase. But where sin increased, grace increased all the more, so that, just as sin reigned in death, so also grace might reign through righteousness to bring eternal life through Jesus Christ our Lord."

Lord, this is so beautifully explained. *"Yes Shirley, this explains My birth and My death on the cross and that is why I chose this Scripture to be included in this work."* Yes Lord. *"Now Listen carefully."* Yes Lord.

"It is in Me and by Me that one is saved. No one comes to My Father but by Me. I am the Way, the Truth and the Life. I am life eternal and this is given to you by grace and not by the law. Come now while grace still abounds. Come for the time is now!"

Time: 1:32 p.m.

"Go to Romans 4:24 & 25: "But also to us, to whom God will credit righteousness – for us who believe in him who raised Jesus Christ our Lord from the dead. He was delivered over to death for our sins and was raised to life for our justification."

"Go to Psalm 25:11, "For the sake of your name, O Lord, forgive my iniquity, though it is great."

"Shirley all I ask is this; come to Me in repentance that I may forgive your sins and that is easily done with a humble heart. Acknowledge that you are a sinner. Come now, while there is still time. Go to Matthew 18:1 – 4,

"At that time the disciples came to Jesus and asked, 'Who is the greatest in the kingdom of heaven?' He called a little child and had him stand among them. And he said; 'I tell you the truth, unless you change and become like little children, you will never enter the kingdom of heaven. Therefore, whoever humbles himself like this child is the greatest in the kingdom of heaven.'"

The thought came to my mind that humbleness is the opposite of pride. God hates pride and requires us to be humble. *"Yes Shirley humbleness opens the heart. The heart is where all pride is stored."* Yes Lord. Lord, so we must pocket our pride as the saying goes and repent and submit to you. *"Shirley, that is what I ask for, is it so much? There is no place in heaven for pride. Pride brings death but humbleness brings life."* Yes Lord.

Saturday, 18 February, 2012, Time: 9:00 a.m.

"Shirley this is for you. Take the Bible and go to Psalm 138."

"I will praise you, O Lord, with all of my heart; before the 'gods' I will sing your praise. I will bow down toward your holy temple and will praise your name for your love and your faithfulness, for you have exalted above all things Your Name and your Word. When I called, you answered me; You made me bold and stout hearted. May all the kings of the earth Praise you, O Lord, may they sing of the ways of the Lord, for the glory of the Lord is great.

Though the Lord is on high, he looks upon the lowly, but the proud he knows from afar. Though I walk in the midst of trouble, You preserve my life; You stretch out your hand against the anger of my foes, with your right hand you save me. The Lord will fulfill his purpose, for me; your love, O Lord, endures forever—do not abandon the works of your hands."

Thank you Lord it is beautiful and yes, Lord, I will praise you all the days of my life for you have made me what I am today, like clay in the potter's hand. *"Let us begin."* Yes Lord.

"The Spirit of the Lord is in those that know Me. The wind blows, you feel it but you cannot see it, so it is with the Holy Spirit of God. Go to Romans 8:24 – 27:

"For in this hope we were saved. But hope that is seen is no hope at all. Who hopes for what he already has? But if we hope for what we do not yet have, we wait for it patiently. In the same way, the Spirit helps us in our weakness. We do not know what we ought to pray for, but the Spirit himself intercedes for us with groans that words cannot express. And he who searches our hearts knows the mind of the Spirit, because the Spirit intercedes for the saints in accordance with God's will."

"The Spirit of the Lord descended upon those who gathered in the upper room like fire. From that day until now the Spirit is in those who know My voice. He is with each one. He gathers them in and teaches them what is to come. He comforts them. He reveals the Word to them. He is the one I spoke of to My disciples when I told them I was going.

Go to Romans 8:5 – 8:

"Those who live according to the sinful nature have their minds set on what that nature desires, but those who live in accordance with the Spirit have their minds set on what the Spirit desires. The mind of sinful man is death, but the mind controlled by the Spirit is life and peace; the sinful mind is hostile to God. It does not submit to God's law, nor can it do so. Those controlled by the sinful nature cannot please God."

"*Go to Romans 8: 9b,*
"And if anyone does not have the Spirit of Christ, he does not belong to Christ."

"Shirley, Listen carefully." Yes Lord.*"My offer stands firm—come now and taste the goodness of God. It is free. All you need to do is put off your pride and set aside your arrogance and come in humbleness before Me. I have so much to give you, come and taste the goodness of God. Come while there is still time."*

Lord, the world seeks other spirits and serves other gods, can they not see that there is only one true Spirit—the Holy Spirit of God and the Creator of Heaven and Earth! *"Shirley, the road is narrow and few find it. The enemy has placed many paths of spirituality before them."* Yes Lord, but surely with some level of reason they must see the confusion. *"Shirley man has reached the level of arrogance where they see all this, and in their arrogance they refuse to search for Me. Instead in their pride they say there is no God or my god is the right god. That is why I say, in arrogance and in pride they fall!"* Yes Lord, I am not a university graduate, but I am not foolish. I searched for You Lord within my limited level of reason. Lord in my search to find You, I did research other religions and the esoteric and with my average intelligence I could see that all roads do not lead to God but only to confusion, in fact I found organized chaos.
"Yes Shirley I have already said that the enemy has placed many paths of spirituality before them." Yes Lord it is so disturbing to see wonderful people being misled so easily because they have become arrogant and the enemy has their minds. The Scripture in 2 Corinthians 4: 4 came to mind, "The god of this age has blinded the minds of unbelievers; so that they cannot see the light of the gospel of the glory of Christ, who is the image of God."

"Shirley, it is pride and arrogance that has allowed their minds to be blinded. Pride is the downfall of mankind just as it was the downfall of Satan. So as long as man stands in pride he is blinded."

Yes Lord, I see this now and I realize why You are calling man to become humble. I understand why You referred to Job earlier on. Lord, Satan is only able to blind the minds of those who walk in arrogance and in pride. That is why You said right in the beginning that arrogance and pride has reached its fill. It has reached the nostrils of God. Lord I so realize now that without becoming humble and submitting to You and receiving the Holy Spirit, man can never know You.

"Yes Shirley and as long as pride controls him, he can never know Me." Yes Lord, it all comes down to pride. Lord this is the lesson man must learn. *"Yes Shirley as long as pride controls him, he is lost."* All I can say is, yes Lord. *"And I say this to all, My offer still stands. Come and taste the goodness of God while there is still time!"*

Sunday, 19 February, 2012, Time: 9:40 a.m.

"Shirley, Listen carefully." Yes Lord. *"I will begin with this Word today. I have seen the hearts of men and I say to you today, turn away from evil, search your hearts and seek Me while I can still be found. I am that I am! It is Me the Lord God Almighty speaking to you. I have so much to say to you if you will turn from your sin and follow Me. Do you not see that I laid My life down for you! I am that I am! I bring warning to you of stubborn hearts as I do not want one person to perish in sin. I have so much more for you. Come follow Me while there is still time. "I have begun with the final countdown. Time is short and I call out to all who will Listen and hear what I am saying. Turn from your evil ways and seek Me with your whole heart and if you do this, you will find Me. I stand ready to receive you into My Kingdom. I know there are many who seek God but seek in the wrong places. You can only find Me with your heart. Your heart is the entry. If you will humble yourself before Me with a searching heart, you will find Me. Is that a difficult thing to do? I have made it easy for you. You do not need to seek God through any other means, just with your heart. I call out to you and I say to you, come! Come and kneel before Me and call on My Name and I will hear you. My Word says; whosoever calls on My Name will be saved. This is a covenant I have with man. I hung on the tree and died for your sin. I stand ready to receive you. Your sin is covered by My blood. You can be washed and made clean. My blood that poured out is for your sin.*

"I call you out today and have been calling you since I paid the price for your sin. I am holy and sin separates us. Come now and be washed by My blood. The price is paid. Come and be made righteous before God. I am King of kings and I am Lord of lords. There is none other. No one can enter heaven but by Me. I am the High Priest. I am the Holy One.

"The day will come soon when I cannot be found. I say again, come now while there is still time. Open the door that I knock on. The door to your heart and let Me in. I stand ready to come in. I will come in if you open the door. My heart cries out to your heart. Please invite me in. Come let us meet that you may know Me. Go to Psalm 123:

"I lift up my eyes to you, to you whose throne is in heaven.

As the eyes of slaves look to the hand of their master,
As the eyes of a maid look to the hand of her mistress,
So our eyes look to the Lord our God till he shows us his mercy.

Have mercy on us, O Lord, have mercy on us,
For we have endured much contempt. We have endured much ridicule from the proud, Much contempt from the arrogant."

"Shirley I have seen the suffering under the hand of the arrogant and the proud. I have seen the pain and anguish it causes those that have nowhere to run. They treat people with contempt. Shirley, unless they come to Me in humbleness their pride has spoken for them. Those who suffer by the hand of the arrogant—I call upon you to come to Me with your door open and invite Me in. Come and receive mercy while grace abounds. Go to Romans 13:8 – 14:

"Let no debt remain outstanding, except the continuing debt to love one another, for he who loves his fellow man has fulfilled the law. The commandments, 'Do not commit adultery,' 'do not murder,' 'do not steal,' 'do not covet,' and whatever other commandment there may be, are summed up in this one rule: 'Love your neighbor as yourself.' Love does no harm to its neighbor. Therefore love is the fulfillment of the law. And do this, understanding the present time. The hour has come for you to wake up from your slumber, because our salvation is nearer now than when we first believed. The night is nearly over; the day is almost here. So let us put aside the deeds of darkness, and put on the armor of light. Let us behave decently, as in the daytime, not in orgies and drunkenness, not in sexual immorality and debauchery, not in dissension and jealousy. Rather clothe yourselves with the Lord Jesus Christ, and do not think about how to gratify the desires of the sinful nature."

"Your sinful nature is stored in your heart. Whatever is in your heart will become your life. Come give Me your heart that I may change it and turn it from a heart of stone to a heart of flesh."

Monday, 20 February, 2012, Time 10:15 a.m.

"Shirley, this is the day the Lord has made. It is the day of warning to the people on earth. Shirley many see and fear the year 2012." Yes Lord. *"Shirley, I am in control. It will be as it is written in My Word. The birth pains have begun and the time of great sorrow is coming. Go to Revelation 12:17:*

"Then the dragon was enraged at the woman and went off to make war against the rest of her offspring – those who obey God's commandments and hold to the testimony of Jesus."

"We have entered these times and since the beginning of the church, war has come against the saints. Those who are Mine must stand in faith for the time for war as never before, has begun. You will be hated and you will be condemned because of your testimony for Me. The arrogance of the arrogant will grow stronger therefore, My own must stand in faith. Know that I am in control. Know that it will be as it is written. The gates of hell cannot prevail against My Word. The world will pass away but My Word will never pass away. My Word is the same Yesterday, today and forever!"

Time: 1:55 p.m.

"Shirley, do not fear for I am with you." Thank you Lord.
"Write this down carefully." Yes Lord. *"All those who are Mine are more than conquerors. Shirley, now go to Psalm 93:*
"The Lord reigns, he is robed in majesty, the Lord is robed in majesty and is armed with strength. The world is firmly established; it cannot be moved. Your throne was established long ago; you are from all eternity. The seas have lifted up, O Lord, the seas have lifted up their voice; the seas have lifted up their pounding waves. Mightier than the thunder of the great waters, mightier than the breakers of the sea—the Lord on high is mighty. Your statutes stand firm; holiness adorns your house for endless days O Lord."

"All who know Me know that I am Holy and Eternal. They stand as mortal men before Me. I am coming soon and what can mortal man do to Me, nothing, for I am God. I am in control. How can a created man come against Me? How can his wisdom surpass Mine? I am the Creator of heaven and earth, so what can man do to Me?" Yes Lord, how can they stand against you? *"Shirley, I came to give life eternal. I came to bring hope. I came to bring salvation. I came and offered My life for mankind and yet they see Me not."* Yes Lord. *"Shirley only the humble see Me."* Yes Lord.
"Shirley, go to Isaiah 46:9 – 13:

"Remember the former things, those of long ago, I am God, and there is no other; I am God, and there is none like me. I make known the end from the beginning, from ancient times, what is still to come. I say: My purpose will stand, and I will do all that I please. From the east I summon a bird of prey; from a far-off land, a man to fulfill my purpose. What I have said, that will I bring about; what I have planned, that will I do. Listen to me, you stubborn-hearted, you who are far from righteousness. I am bringing my righteousness near, it is not far away; and my salvation will not be delayed. I will grant salvation to Zion, My splendor to Israel."

Yes Lord, You are coming. *"Shirley I come soon, sooner than many think. This time I am not coming as a Lamb to be slaughtered, but I come as a Lion. I am coming to fulfil My Word and I am coming to take all that is Mine."* Yes Lord and nothing will stop this. *"Shirley, again I say, what can mortal man do to Me?"* Nothing Lord! *"You are right Shirley, nothing! Shirley, I come for those with a pure heart and clean hands. These are the hearts that have been washed by My blood. These are the hearts that are Mine."* Yes Lord. Lord, many believe that as long as they are saved they will go to heaven. *"Shirley, many who are saved, lead double lives. They have been fooled but I am not fooled. Now is the time for those sheep to come back to Me. They must repent and return to Me so that I can forgive them. They must do this now while mercy and grace abounds."* Yes Lord.

"Shirley, My sheep know My voice and I say to those who have grown cold, come and come now for you do not know the time or the hour that I return. I come as a thief in the night and unless they turn from their sin, the door will be shut." Yes Lord. *"I have many rewards for those who will come and stand before Me with a pure heart and clean hands. Much awaits those who will come. My Father's house has many mansions and no mind can conceive what is waiting for them. But know this, God is not fooled."* Yes Lord. *"So then, Shirley tell My people, 'Come now and prepare for the Lord comes soon.'"* Yes Lord, I will tell people. *"Shirley, My church sleeps. I have given them My Word, but they sleep. Shirley, I am giving*

them this Word through you now and do you think they will Listen?" Lord I pray that they will. *"Shirley, even My shepherds sleep!"* Lord I have seen this. *"I say today as I call upon all My shepherds—prepare your sheep for the time is short! Go and find your lost sheep and bring them in. I call on My shepherds, make straight the path for the Lord. Now is the time!"* **Tuesday, 21 February, 2012, Time: 9: 10 a.m.**

"As I speak to you now please Listen carefully and please make sure you write all down." Yes Lord. *"I come as a thief in the night. Let that be a warning to you. You will not know the time or the hour. So then this is what I say to you – be prepared. Unless you are prepared you will find the door shut tight."*
The anointing falls heavily on me. I wait on the Lord.

"This is for the people of the world. I say to you today, turn from your wicked ways for unless you turn to Me you will fall never to rise again. I bring this warning to you and I say to you; open your ears and hear My voice for I speak to you. Do not hide behind your intellect for it will let you fall. I am beyond your intellect. Remember, My thoughts are not your thoughts and My ways are not your ways. I will fulfil My Word to the last Word. This is My warning to you. Seek Me while you still have time. My grace abounds. My mercy is at your doorstep. This is My last call. Will you Listen and hear what I am saying. Repent for now is the time."

"Shirley this is for you. Be prepared for many will come against you but know that I am with you and in you." Yes Lord. *"Go to Psalm 58,*

"Do you rulers indeed speak justly? Do you judge uprightly among men? No, in your heart you devise injustice, and your hands mete out violence on the earth. Even from birth the wicked go astray;
from the womb they are wayward and speak lies. Their venom is like the venom of a snake, like a cobra that has stopped its ears that will not heed the tune of the charmer, however skilful the enchanter may be. Break the teeth in their mouths, O God, tear out, O Lord, the fangs of the lions! Let them vanish like water that flows away; when they draw the bow, let their arrows be blunted. Like a slug melting away as it moves along, like a stillborn child, may they not see the sun. Before your pots can feel the heat of the thorns—whether they be green or dry—the wicked will be swept away. The righteous will be glad when they are avenged, when they bathe their feet in the blood of the wicked. Then men will say, 'Surely the righteous still are rewarded; Surely there is a God who judges the earth.'"

"Shirley I come to take those who are Mine and I come to judge this world. The earth will be glad for it reels under the sin of man. I come to judge this world filled with people who have no regard for God. You have turned your back on Me, your Creator. But I say to you, I come soon to judge as I am the Righteous Judge. Shirley, go to Psalm 11:

"In the Lord I take refuge. How then can you say to me; 'Flee like a bird to your mountain.' For look, the wicked bend their bows; they set their arrows against the strings to shoot from the shadows at the upright in heart. When the foundations are being destroyed, what can the righteous do? The Lord is in his holy temple; the Lord is on his heavenly throne. He observes the sons of men; His eyes examine them. The Lord examines the righteous, but the wicked and those who love violence his soul hates. On the wicked he will rain fiery coals and burning sulphur, a scorching wind will be their lot. For the Lord is righteous, He loves justice; upright men will see his face."

"Shirley, the world does not know Me, only My own know Me." Yes Lord. *"They have become arrogant in all that they do. In that arrogance, they will fall."* Yes Lord. *"Go to Psalm 98:2 & 8 – 9:*

"The Lord has made his salvation known and revealed his righteousness to the nations. Let the rivers clap their hands, let the mountains sing together for joy; let them sing before the Lord, for he comes to judge the earth. He will judge the world in righteousness and the peoples with equity."

"Listen, you nations of earth, I am the Righteous Judge and there is none other. I am the Beginning and the End, the Alpha and the Omega. Do you hear? Shirley, write down only what I say; be careful." Yes Lord. *"Since the beginning I have spoken to the people on earth through My chosen ones. I have given them a Word to bring to the people. So it is time now to bring this Word to you, the people of this world. I am speaking to you today. Go to Isaiah 56:9 – 12:* God's Accusation against the Wicked.

"Come, all you beasts of the field, come and devour, all you beasts of the forest! Israel's watchmen are blind, they all lack knowledge; they are all mute dogs, they cannot bark; they lie around and dream, they love to sleep. They are dogs with mighty appetites; they never have enough. They are shepherds who lack understanding, they all turn to their own way, each seeks his own gain. 'Come,' each one cries, 'let me get wine! Let us drink our fill of beer! And tomorrow will be like today, or even better.'"

"See how I spoke to the Shepherds of Israel. Now I speak to you who say; 'I am a pastor'; 'I am a prophet'; 'I am a teacher.' Let Me tell you, unless you turn to Me in repentance for leading My sheep astray, I will come and devour you. Do you not know that you will lead My sheep into the pit! Repent and come back to your first love. You the ones that have turned My church into a circus. I bring warning to you—do this now while there is still time. Are you not false prophets? Did you not read My warning to the false prophets?"
The anointing falls heavier again on me.

"Yes you who know Me and serve My people in the church. Return to Me and gather your sheep and bring them into the pasture of the Lord Jesus Christ. You will stand accountable. Be warned for I have spoken! Prepare My people to meet their Lord. This is your calling this is what I called you to do. Do it now, while there is still time."

Time: 1:40 p.m.

"All those who call on My Name will be saved. I say this to you – come now before Me while there is still time. Mercy awaits you and grace abounds. I am Arisen! And I am Alive! And I am that I am!"
"Shirley, Listen carefully now." Yes Lord.
"Go to Matthew 24:30 – 35: (Jesus speaking)

"At that time the Sign of the Son of Man will appear in the sky, and all the nations of the earth will mourn. They will see the Son of Man coming on the clouds of the sky, with power and great glory. And he will send his angels with a loud trumpet call, and they will gather his elect from the four winds, from one end of the heavens to the other. Now learn this lesson from the fig tree; as soon as its twigs get tender and its leaves come out, you know that summer is near. Even so, when you see all these things, you know that it is near, right at the door. I tell you the truth this generation will certainly not pass away until these things have happened. Heaven and earth will pass away, but my words will never pass away."

"Yes I am coming again! Shirley I can see you are troubled." Yes Lord. *"I have heard your prayer. Know this, I have chosen you to do this. Do you remember that I called you many years ago?"* Yes Lord. *"So then know this—My prophets know My voice. They hear Me and I them. I am in you as you are in Me. This is a difficult calling but remember I have prepared you."* Yes Lord. *"What do you fear?"* Lord I am afraid that I do not hear you as I should and I want the Words to be correct. *"Shirley, you have been trained over many years."* Yes Lord. *"Therefore, let Me speak through you as I have been doing. Remember I spoke through you the last time you ministered?"* Yes Lord. *"It was Me."* Yes Lord. *"So then I am doing the same thing."* Yes Lord. *"Go to Psalm 128."* Thank you Lord. *"Peace be with you Shirley."* Thank you Lord. *"Go to Romans 15: 5 & 6:*

"May the God who gives endurance and encouragement give you a spirit of unity among yourselves as you follow Christ Jesus, so that with one heart and mouth you may glorify the God and Father of our Lord Jesus Christ." Thank you I am at peace and I thank you that You always give me assurance.

Wednesday, 22 February, 2012, Time: 9:00 a.m.

"Shirley, today is a special day." Yes, Lord, it is my late brother's birthday. *"Now as we begin, keep calm and Listen carefully."*
Yes Lord. *"Go to Romans 10:9 – 13:*

"That if you confess with your mouth, 'Jesus is Lord' and believe in your heart that God raised him from the dead, you will be saved. For it is with your heart that you believe and are justified, and it is with your mouth that you confess and are saved. As the Scripture says, 'Anyone who trusts in him will never be put to shame.' For there is no difference between Jew and Gentile—the same Lord is Lord of all and richly blesses all who call on him. For, everyone who calls on the name of the Lord will be saved."

"So it is with anyone who calls on the Lord. Here I am. I stand at the door of your heart. I wait patiently for you to open the door. Shirley, go to Romans 16:25 – 27:

"Now to him who is able to establish you by my gospel and the proclamation of Jesus Christ, according to the revelation of the mystery hidden for long ages past, but now revealed and made known through the prophetic writing by the command of the eternal God, so that all nations might believe and obey him—to the only wise God be glory forever through Jesus Christ! Amen."

"I am the Lord Jesus Christ. I say to you all, as My Word says in the Bible, I will come soon and I call on those who will hear My message, come while there is still time for the world heads along the path of destruction. Go to Isaiah 35:4 & 8:

"Say to those with fearful hearts, 'Be strong, do not fear; Your God will come, He will come with vengeance, with divine retribution he will come to save you.' And a highway will be there; it will be called the Way of Holiness. The unclean will not journey on it; it will be for those who walk in that way; wicked fools will not go about on it."

"Listen carefully." Yes Lord. The anointing falls heavier on my head and the back of my neck. *"I am about to bring My sword, My Word as it is written to its end. The world scoffs at My Word but that same scoffing will turn to tears. This is what I say to those who will hear My Word. Not tears of joy but tears of terror. Yes you scoffers, you will cry bitter tears. It is as it is written. So be it."* The heavy anointing slowly lifts and I feel the determination of the Lord.

Thursday, 23 February, 2012, Time: 1:50 p.m.

"Listen carefully that you may know the Words." Yes Lord.
"Go to Psalm 1,"

"Blessed is the man who does not walk in the
Counsel of the wicked
Or stand in the way of sinners
Or sit in the seat of the mockers,
But his delight is in the law of the Lord,
And on his law he meditates day and night.
He is like a tree planted by the streams of water,
Which yields its fruit in season
And whose leaf does not wither.
Whatever he does prospers.
Not so the wicked!
They are like chaff that the wind blows away.
Therefore the wicked will not stand in judgment,
Nor sinners in the assembly of the righteous For the Lord watches over the way of the righteous, But the way of the wicked will perish."

"Shirley I want you to write this down carefully." Yes Lord.
"I understand the ways of the world. I see how it progresses. I know its beginning and I know its end. Now I tell you the truth— unless you repent you will perish. Unless you turn from your sin, you will perish, unless you turn away from false gods you will perish. I am the Way, the Truth and the Life. No one comes to the Father but by Me.

"Go and call all your friends and come and sit with Me. Let Me speak to you all with these Words while there is still time. Tell your friends that you have seen these Words. Let your friends tell their friends that they have seen these Words for the time is short and destruction awaits and will come for I the Lord Jesus Christ have said so. Do not say you have not been warned. I have brought all that I need and I have done all that has to be done. The preparation is in the fold of My Father's hand. Let this be a warning. Go to Romans 14:11 & 12, it is written:

"'As surely as I live,' says the Lord, 'every knee will bow before me; every tongue will confess to God' so then, each of us will give an account of himself to God."

"Now I say to you—stand ready to receive what you have sown. If it is good, then you have sown wisely but if it is evil, then you have sown foolishly. But there is still time! Come now while mercy and grace abound. Go to John 4:12 – 14,

"'Are you greater than our father Jacob, who gave us the well and drank from it himself, as did also his sons and his flocks and herds?' Jesus answered, 'everyone who drinks this water will be thirsty again, but whoever drinks the water I give him will never thirst. Indeed, the water I give him will become in him a spring of water welling up to eternal life.'"

"For those of you who thirst after the truth, come to Me for I am the Way, the Truth and the Life. The world seeks truth but it can only be found in Me."

Friday, 24 February, 2012, Time: 8:15 a.m. 57

"Shirley, this is for you today. I have seen your concern but know this; this is My work and by My hand therefore, I will bring it into the world." Yes Lord, thank you. *"Now Listen carefully as I speak to you."* Yes Lord. *"Many do not believe that I speak to My children. But I say to you, My sheep know My voice. I lead My sheep in many ways. They hear My voice because they spend time with Me. Each one has the Holy Spirit within. I hear their words and they hear Mine. If you open the door to your heart and invite Me in, then we eat together. We have wonderful fellowship. This is for all My sheep. I say to you today, come and eat with Me! I have begun with this work to reach My children and I say to you, come close to Me for now is the time. Keep your lamps filled with oil for you know that I come as a thief in the night to take those of My own. Go to John 4:23 & 24,* Jesus speaking,

"Yet a time is coming and has now come when the true worshipers will worship the Father in Spirit and Truth, for they are the kind of worshipers the Father seeks. God is spirit and his worshipers must worship in Spirit and in Truth."

"For soon comes a time when the harvest will come. The wheat and the chaff will be separated and those for Me will come to Me and those against Me will be gathered into bundles and thrown into the fiery furnace. This is a warning to all. Go to Revelation 3:15 – 19,

"I know your deeds, that you are neither cold nor hot. I wish you were either one or the other! So, because you are lukewarm— neither hot nor cold—I am about to spit you out of my mouth. You say, 'I am rich; I have acquired wealth and do not need a thing.' But you do not realize that you are wretched, pitiful, poor, blind and naked. I counsel you to buy from me gold refined in the fire, so you can become rich; and white clothes to wear, so you can cover your shameful nakedness; and salve to put on your eyes, so you can see. Those whom I love I rebuke and discipline. So be earnest and repent."

"Go to Revelation 3:21 & 22,"

"To him who overcomes, I will give the right to sit with me on my throne, just as I overcame and sat down with my Father on his throne. He who has an ear, let him hear what the Spirit says to the churches."

Yes Lord, I pray that they will hear. *"Shirley, now go to Revelation 22:16,"*

"I, Jesus, have sent my angel to give you this testimony for the churches. I am the Root and the Offspring of David, and the Bright Morning Star."

Saturday, 25 February, 2012, Time: 5:38 p.m.

"Be careful as you write, make each Word count as they are Mine." Yes Lord. *"I am beginning with this Word. The time has come for the Word to be fulfilled as it is written. All who know Me will know that it is Me speaking. I have set My anointing over these Words in such a way that it will never be returned void. Listen My people, Listen to what I am saying to the church today. I am doing this so that there can be no confusion among you. Hear My Words for they are true and faithful. I have this Word for you; come and stand in My presence so that you may receive. Let your heart be hungry for Me. Let it be filled to*

overflowing with living water for now is the time. I am calling you in. Come now for it is time. I have said this many times so that you may see the urgency of the time you live in. My Word is for you. The prophet's Words are for you. The Bible is for you and now I speak to you. Go to Isaiah 26:20 & 21,

"Go my people, enter your rooms and shut the doors behind you; hide yourself for a little while until his wrath has passed by. See, the Lord is coming out of his dwelling to punish the people of the earth for their sins. The earth will disclose the blood shed upon her; she will conceal her slain no longer."

"Do not be afraid but rather come to Me in humbleness that I may receive you. Let us walk together into the light of the God Most High. Come and receive what is stored up for you. See I come to take those who are Mine. Come for now is the time!"

Sunday, 26 February, 2012, Time: 9:32 a.m.

Shirley, Listen carefully." Yes Lord. *"Go to Romans 6:7 – 14,*

"Because anyone who has died, has been freed from sin. Now if we died with Christ, we believe that we will also live with him. For we know that since Christ was raised from the dead, he cannot die again; death no longer has mastery over him. The death he died, he died to sin once for all; but the life he lives, he lives to God. In the same way, count yourselves dead to sin but alive to God in Christ Jesus. Therefore do not let sin reign in your mortal body so that you obey its evil desires. Do not offer the parts of your body to sin, as instruments of wickedness, but rather offer yourselves to God, as those who have been brought from death to life; and offer the parts of your body to him as instruments of righteousness. For sin shall not be your master because you are not under law, but under grace.
"Do not live your lives as the world lives. Live rather to God as sin leads to death. Remember I have paid the price. Come now and Listen to what the Lord says for I am giving you this to warn you that time is short and I come soon. Come now while grace abounds. Go to Romans 8:14 – 17,

"Because those who are led by the Spirit of God are sons of God. For you did not receive a Spirit that makes you a slave again to fear, but you received the spirit of sonship. And by him we cry, 'Abba, Father.' The Spirit himself testifies with our spirit that we are God's children. Now if we are children, then we are heirs – heirs of God and co-heirs with Christ, if indeed we share in his sufferings in order that we may also share in his glory."

"See now and understand that I the Lord have given you all you need. Come now and obey Me for I am the Way, the Truth and the Life. No one comes to the Father but by Me. Shirley, Listen carefully." Yes Lord. *"I say to the world, your time is short. You labor in vain. You have become like sheep without a shepherd. Like a headless chicken. You have no direction neither do you seek it. You have turned your back on God. You have become orphans. You who say, 'I am man and I live by my rules.' But know this—I am that I am! Soon you will know that I am that I am. This is what the Lord God says to you—I come soon!"*

Time: 7:40 p.m.

A heavy anointing falls on me. *"Shirley, go in My Name and in My Power and in My Authority. I have prepared this for you. I have given you all you need."* Yes Lord. *"I will come in power to you for I have much to tell you and show you."* Yes Lord. *"Do not let anything distract you."* Yes Lord.
"Stay close to Me." Yes, Lord. *"Shirley this is for you—you have been called to do this."* Yes Lord.

Monday, 27 February, 2012, Time: 9:15 a.m.

"Shirley, come now let us begin." Yes Lord. *"I have come to give this warning to all. To those that will open their ears and hear what the Lord is saying to the world today. Let it be known that I, the Lord Jesus Christ am giving this Word for those who will Listen. I am that I am. Shirley, go to Romans 10:19 & 20,*

"Again I ask: did Israel not understand? First, Moses says, 'I will make you envious by those who are not a nation; I will make you angry by a nation that has no understanding,' and Isaiah boldly says, 'I was found by those who did not seek me; I revealed myself to those who did not ask for me.'"

"See, I have revealed Myself to all nations. I am found by those who seek Me with their whole heart. I am here, I stand at the door to the hearts of all nations. I am found if you seek Me with your heart. Seek Me now while I may be found. Shirley, go to Psalm 49:7 – 15,

"No man can redeem the life of another or give to God a ransom for him—the ransom for a life is costly, no payment is ever enough—that he should live on forever and not see decay. For all can see that wise men die, the foolish and the senseless alike perish and leave their wealth to others. Their tombs will remain their houses forever, their dwellings for endless generations, though they had named lands after themselves. But man, despite his riches, does not endure;he is like the beasts that perish. This is the fate of those who trust in themselves, and of their followers, who approve their sayings. Like sheep they are destined for the grave, and death will feed on them. The upright will rule over them in the morning; their forms will decay in the grave, far from their princely mansions, but God will redeem my life from the grave; He will surely take me to himself."

"Come now you who say you are wise, who say I am rich, I am in need of nothing—are you rich? Do you own eternal life? No one can pay your ransom—only you can pay this ransom with your life—that is, your life redeemed by Me. I say to you, come now while grace abounds. I am the Redeemer, I am your Salvation, I am the Way, the Truth, and the Life. No one comes to the Father but by Me. Shirley." Yes Lord *"Now comes the time when you must Listen very carefully for I am taking you into the Word that will require complete obedience."* Yes Lord. *"Now I want you to put all aside until this is done."* Yes Lord. *"Will you do this?"* I will Lord. *"So then we will do this together."* Yes Lord. *"Good for I am with you and in you. Do not fear the Word."* Yes Lord I will not fear. *"Good for fear will keep you from hearing Me."* I understand Lord. *"Shirley, you have heard correctly."* Thank you Lord. *"Now go to Daniel 7,* (Daniel's Dream of The Four Beasts). I had not read the book of Daniel for quite some time so I spent time reading it again and we did not continue until the next day.

Tuesday, 28 February, 2012, Time: 9:52 a.m.

"Now let us begin. Listen carefully." Yes Lord. *"Go to Daniel 7:16 – 27,*

"I approached one of those standing there and asked him the true meaning of all this. So he told me and gave me the interpretation of these things; 'The four great beasts are four kingdoms that will rise from the earth. But the saints of the Most High will receive the kingdom and will possess it forever—yes, forever and ever.' Then I wanted to know the true meaning of the fourth beast, which was different from all the others and most terrifying, with its iron teeth and bronze claws—the beast that crushed and devoured its victims and trampled underfoot whatever was left. I also wanted to know about the ten horns on its head and about the other horn that came up, before which three of them fell—the horn that looked more imposing than the others and that had eyes and a mouth that spoke boastfully. As I watched, this horn was waging war against the saints and defeating them, until the Ancient of Days came and pronounced judgment in favor of the saints of the Most High, and the time came when they possessed the Kingdom.

He gave me the explanation: 'The fourth beast is a fourth kingdom that will appear on earth. It will be different from all the other kingdoms and will devour the whole earth, trampling it down and crushing it. The ten horns are ten kings who will come from this kingdom. After them another king will arise, different from the earlier ones; he will subdue three kings.

"He will speak against the Most High and oppress his saints and try to change the set times and the laws. The saints will be handed over to him for a time, times and half a time. But the court will sit, and his power will be taken away and completely destroyed forever. Then the sovereignty, power and greatness of the kingdoms under the whole heaven will be handed over to the saints, the people of the Most High. His kingdom will be an everlasting kingdom, and all rulers will worship and obey him."
"Shirley now I want you to go to Revelation 13:8 – 10,

"All the inhabitants of the earth will worship the beast—all whose names have not been written in the book of life belonging to the Lamb that was slain from the creation of the world. He who has an ear, let him hear. If anyone is to go into captivity, into captivity he will go. If anyone is to be killed with the sword, with the sword he will be killed. This calls for patient endurance and faithfulness on the part of the saints."

"Shirley now Listen carefully, all those who worship the beast will be cut off from the Most High God." Yes Lord. *"There will be no repentance for it will be too late for them."* Yes Lord. *"Go to 1 Peter 1:24,*

"For, all men are like grass, and all their glory is like the flowers of the field; the grass withers and the flowers fall, but the Word of the Lord stands forever."

I lose focus and the Lord tells me to go out for a while. I am now back and I wait on the Lord. *"Shirley, now Listen carefully."* Yes Lord. *"Go to Revelation 8:1 & 2,* The Seventh Seal and the Golden Censer:

"When he opened the seventh seal, there was silence in heaven for about half an hour. And I saw the seven angels who stand before God, and to them were given seven trumpets."

"This is what the Lord God Almighty says to you; the time has come and is upon you now for the seventh seal to be poured out upon the earth. Those who have ears let him hear. All is ready for the time spoken of and written about is about to fall into its place. The whole world stands ready to receive that which it has stored up. The end of days is upon the world. The time of great tribulation as never before is about to be released. Man is about to find his destiny. People of earth will know that I am the Creator and the Beginning and the End. To those of you that will Listen, I say to you now, 'Listen for it is time to Listen.' Shirley, go to Revelation 9,"
Yes Lord, I have opened it up. *"Now Listen carefully."* Yes Lord. *"Will these arrogant people who scoff at My Word Listen?"* Lord I do not know. *"Well go to verse 20 & 21,*

"The rest of mankind that were not killed by these plagues still did not repent of the work of their hands; they did not stop worshiping demons, and idols of gold, silver, bronze, stone and wood—idols that cannot see or hear or walk. Nor did they repent of their murders, their magic arts, their sexual immorality or their thefts."

Lord, people are stubborn. *"Shirley, since the beginning I have pleaded with man. I have sent My prophets to bring warning. I came so that those who will Listen will be given unto salvation. I paid the price for sin. I have sent out My laborers, I have given people shepherds. I have given My Holy Book. Now I call out again to those who will open their ears and hear My voice. I have given warning to the world. But those that will not Listen will receive what they have sown. Rebellious people, stubborn people, arrogant people, all those who are filled will pride will fall never to be picked up."*

I am upset and leave for a while. I am trembling with fear for the world and for my family and myself. Doubt starts creeping into my mind and my thoughts are racing. Am I really doing this, has the Lord really called *me*—me a quiet reserved person? I am shaken as I realize that the time the Bible speaks about and Christians from the time of Christ have been waiting for and searching the Word for over 2,000 years is upon us. I am concerned and as reality and the seriousness of this Word sets in, I start questioning myself. Doubt and fear run wild in my mind. Am I truly hearing this? Am I a false prophet? Panic for the people of earth strikes my heart. After some time I calm down and the confusion lifts. I pull myself together. Calmly I think and I decide that I am hearing this and I am writing this down. I know the Lord is in me and I am in Him. I gather myself together and return fully aware that the Lord hears all my thoughts.

Time: 1:40 p.m.

"You are upset Shirley." Yes, Lord. *"Why?"* Lord, I just pray that I have heard all your Words correctly. Lord, you know that I am afraid of being a false prophet. *"Shirley, you were called to do this."* Yes Lord. *"Do you think I would call a false prophet?"* No Lord, You would not. *"Do you not know that I have been with you?"* Yes Lord I know You are with me. *"Do you see that fear will stop you from hearing My voice?"* I understand Lord, I became confused. I remember that the Lord had warned me earlier as He knew I would fear. Please forgive me Lord. *"Shirley, know this; I know your fears as I know you."* Yes Lord, I understand. *"You are forgiven."* Thank you Lord. *"Now Listen carefully."* Yes Lord. *"I have begun this work in you for My purpose."* Yes Lord. *"So then, peace be upon you."* Thank you Lord. The anointing lifts and I close off for the day.

Wednesday, 29 February, 2012, Time: 11:00 a.m.

"Shirley, wait on Me as I give you the Word." Yes Lord. *"Shirley, Listen carefully."* Yes Lord. *"Go to Romans 1:18 – 25,* God's Wrath Against Mankind.

"The wrath of God is being revealed from heaven against all the godlessness and wickedness of men who suppress the truth by their wickedness, since what may be known about God is plain to them, because God has made it plain to them. For since the creation of the world God's invisible qualities—his eternal power and divine nature— have been clearly seen, being understood from what has been made, so that men are without excuse. For although they knew God, they neither glorified him as God nor gave thanks to him, but their thinking became futile and their foolish hearts were darkened.
Although they claimed to be wise, they became fools and exchanged the glory of the immortal God for images made to look like mortal man and birds and animals and reptiles. Therefore, God gave them over in the sinful desires of their hearts to sexual impurity for the degrading of their bodies with one another. They exchanged the truth of God for a lie, and worshiped and served creative things rather than the Creator—who is forever praised. Amen."

The Lord then said I must stand at my window and look into my garden. He then asked me, *"How* do you know the Creator?" I replied, "I serve the Creator and I know that our creation did not come about without knowledge that is beyond our understanding." I sat down and felt in my heart that the Lord wanted me to share my experience with you. I will begin with this. I grew up with a Christian mother and an atheist father. I attended Sunday School and was confirmed and married in the Methodist Church but never knew I needed to be born again. I only got saved 20 years ago and this is how it happened. In my heart I knew we had a Creator but my dad would remind me often that it was all a lot of nonsense. I was totally confused about God. I did not have peace with this until the day came when I went looking for God. I read up on many religions and visited esoteric fairs and found chaos. I realized that God and the Creator must be the one and same person. You see, as a gardener and animal lover I never doubted that a Creator existed much to my dad's annoyance. One day I was tired of the confusion and I went into my garden and raised my arms and called out to the Creator asking Him to hear me and answer me. I told Him that I could not find Him due to the confusion among all the beliefs in the world. I only want the Creator and I will serve none other. Within a week my life changed. The Lord led my husband and I into a 'born-again' church and we were saved and both our lives changed.

You see, I did what God the Creator is calling out to the world to do. Just call on Him like I did. If He did it for me then He will do it for you. As a keen gardener, I see such great beauty in a garden that is well planned and designed. When I look at a landscape I see how God has planned His gardens, the fauna and the flora all working together. We cannot create a flower. We can only grow them. How does the seed, the soil and the water, know what to do? When the seed, water and the soil meet, they create a plant. It's amazing! Each has its own season. If it is a winter flower, it will lay dormant until the earth cools and each seed grows after its own kind.

The reality is that a great Mind did this. Just look at the variety and the beautiful colors. Flowers grow in all kinds of environments. Another amazing sight, are the fish that live in and around coral reefs. Think about their colors. It just absolutely astounds me. The oceans themselves speak a lot about the Creator. Most magnificent and filled with sea creatures of all kinds, all fulfilling a purpose and feeding millions of people. In fact our oceans are a world within our world. Wow, God gave us two worlds.

One perfect South African morning, I picked a magnificent deep red velvet rose, with little droplets of rain balancing on the perfectly sculptured delicate petals emitting a beautiful fragrance and I took it in to show my father. I asked him if man can make this from scratch. He did not have an answer. I have to stand in awe of our Creator for His choice of designs and colors. I often lift my arms up to the Lord and say 'wow' as I appreciate all that He has given to man. Our planet is magnificent and the sights are breath taking.

One cannot miss the hand of God. Just open your eyes and look at the creation that surrounds you as you pass it by every day, even your pet dog or cat. You know, the sad thing is that most people take the Lord's creation for granted never wondering who did this. Have you ever seen a stallion galloping off into the fields or like us in South Africa, lions on the prowl seeking their prey? I challenge you to seek Him for yourself and with your heart so that you too may know the Creator. Unless you seek Him you will remain ignorant and foolish. Just as the creation is real, so the Creator is real.

God is the Creator of heaven and earth! Do not be foolish but rather come in humbleness before Mighty God as you are a mortal created being just like me. When I went searching for God, I humbled myself and called out to Him. He heard my cry and came and took me by my hand and led me unto salvation.

What our Creator is saying to His human creation is this—'You are without excuse if you deny the work of My hand—My Creation.' Do you know that some people worship the creation and the elements but never look for the Creator? Others serve the energy or the force, but not the Creator. And others serve man by making idols out of them. Unless you give God, the Creator a chance in your life, how can you make a decision not to follow Him? It is like being offered a fantastic job and then deciding to not go for the interview. If you don't go for the interview, how would you know what perks are offered and what the future prospects and benefits would be?

The question I have in my heart for you, the reader, is this: You cannot be the Creator but hypothetically, if you were, how would you feel when your creation scoffs and laughs at you and turns its back on you even after you come down to earth and die on a cross for them so that they won't have to go to hell for their sin? Powerful question—think about it. But I can assure you that we as His creation cannot even begin to understand His love and His patience. He has given this world 2,000 years to find Him since He went to the cross and rose again. Now the Creator is about to return. Please listen and hear His voice now before it is too late.

"Shirley, I have so much stored up for those who will heed My call." Yes Lord. *"I have peace that surpasses all understanding."* Yes Lord I know that peace for it is not a human peace as it transcends our understanding. *"Go to Matthew 6:19 – 21,* (Jesus speaking)

"Do not store up for yourselves treasures on earth, where moth and rust destroy, and where thieves break in and steal. But store up for yourselves treasures in heaven, where moth and rust do not destroy, and where thieves do not break in and steal. For where your treasure is, there your heart will be also."

"For a long time I have waited to call you to do this. Now I want you to Listen well for it is very urgent." Yes Lord. *"I am bringing this Word into the world as it is time."* I will give you all that has been purposed for this."* Yes Lord. *"Go to 1 Peter 4:16 – 19,*

"However, if you suffer as a Christian, do not be ashamed, but praise God that you bear that name. For it is time for judgment to begin with the family of God; and if it begins with us, what will the outcome be for those who do not obey the Gospel of God? And, if it is hard for the righteous to be saved, what will become of the ungodly and the sinner? So then, those who suffer according to God's will, should commit themselves to their faithful Creator and continue to do good."

"Shirley, do you see that all must come to Me in fear and in trembling for I am God. I demand respect and honor. Many do not honor Me. They say, 'I am a Christian,' but where is their respect? I say to all those who say 'I am a Christian,' are you? Do you serve Me as I expect or do you disregard My commands? "Now is the time for you to reach down into your heart and turn away from your hidden sin for I tell you this—nothing is hidden from My sight. All is brought out by My light. To serve Me is to obey Me. To love Me is to obey Me. Get back onto the narrow road that you may be saved. Come and repent that you may be forgiven, come now while there is still time for you do not know the time or the hour that I will return."

Thursday, 1 March, 2012, Time: 8:25 a.m.

"Listen carefully as we continue." Yes Lord. *"The one that comes to Me in repentance will receive forgiveness from their sin. They will become children of the Most High God. My Word is true and faithful. Go to Romans 9:15 – 29,*

"For he says to Moses, 'I will have mercy on whom I have mercy, and I will have compassion on whom I will have compassion.' It does not, therefore, depend on man's desire or effort, but on God's mercy. For the Scripture says to Pharaoh: 'I raised you up for this very purpose, that I might display my power in you and that my name might be proclaimed in all the earth.' Therefore God has mercy on whom he wants to have mercy, and he hardens whom he wants to harden.'

"One of you will say to me; 'Then why does God still blame us? For who resists his will?' But who are you, O man, to talk back to God? Shall what is formed say to him who formed it, 'Why did you make me like this?' Does not the potter have the right to make out of the same lump of clay some pottery for noble purposes and some for common use? What if God, choosing to show his wrath and make his power known, bore with great patience the objects of his wrath—prepared for destruction?

"What if he did this to make the riches of his glory known to the objects of his mercy whom he prepared in advance for glory – even us, who he also called, not only from the Jews but also from the Gentiles? As he says in Hosea:

'I will call them "my people" who are not my people; and I will call her "my loved one" who is not my loved one and, it will happen that in the very place where it was said to them, "You are not my people," they will be called "sons of the living God."' Isaiah cries out concerning Israel; 'Though the number of the Israelites be like the sand by the sea, only a remnant will be saved. For the Lord will carry out His sentence on earth with speed and finality.' "It is just as Isaiah said previously; 'Unless the Lord Almighty had left us descendants, we would have become like Sodom, We would have been like Gomorrah."

"All those who heed My call to repentance will receive salvation. This is the time to come before your God. The world is on a collision course with its destiny. It has rejected My Word and it lives by its own rules. My rules have been set aside and man has in his own image, given birth to his own rules." "Shirley, go to Revelation 7: 9 – 17,"

The Great Multitude in White Robes.

"After this I looked and there before me was a great multitude that no one could count, from every nation, tribe, people and language, standing before the throne and in front of the Lamb. They were wearing white robes and were holding palm branches in their hands. And they cried out in a loud voice: 'Salvation belongs to our God, who sits on the throne, and to the Lamb.' All the angels were standing around the throne and around the elders and the four living creatures. They fell down on their faces before the throne and worshiped God, saying: 'Amen! Praise and glory and wisdom and thanks and honor and power and strength be to our God for ever and ever. Amen!'

"Then one of the elders asked me, 'These in white robes – who are they, and where did they come from?' I answered, 'Sir, you know.' And he said, 'These are they who have come out of the great tribulation; they have washed their robes and made them white in the blood of the Lamb. Therefore, they are before the throne of God and serve him day and night in his temple, and he who sits on the throne will spread his tent over them.' Never again will they hunger; never again will they thirst. The sun will not beat upon them, nor any scorching heat. For the Lamb at the center of the throne will be their shepherd; He will lead them to springs of living water. And God will wipe away every tear from their eyes.
"Shirley, Listen carefully." Yes Lord. *"Understand this: I am Jesus, the Son of Man and the Son of God. I sit at the right hand side of God. I am the One the Scriptures speak about—I am the One the Scripture says of—a child will be born in Bethlehem. I am the One the Scripture speaks of—by His stripes you will be healed. I am the One the Scripture says—'He was taken up in the clouds and He will return in the same way.' I am that I am."*

Friday, 2 March, 2012, Time: 9:24 a.m.

"Listen carefully to what I am saying to you." Yes Lord.
"This will be something different and I need you to Listen carefully." Yes Lord. *"This is the day the Lord has made. Yes I am calling out of the world those who follow other gods. I say to you today; come out of her now. I am calling you now. Babylon will fall and if you are in her you too will fall."*
Lord, many do not understand who Babylon is. *"Yes Shirley that is why I am telling you now."* Yes Lord. *"Babylon is the world system. It is the power that will rule as one. It is the home of all the gods that have infiltrated the world. It is a system that works as one and under one power. It is the downfall of the world. It is in the Scriptures and it is in the world. It is the power of Satan.*

"Now I issue a warning to the world. Come out of her now for now is the time. Do not serve this power because it leads to death. In one hour that power will be broken for I have spoken. If you are part of this power you too will be led into death. Time is short and I come now to warn the people of this world. Come out of her, now! See in one hour she will fall. She will be destroyed for all to see for I the Lord God Almighty have spoken. Go to Revelation 16,"
The Seven Bowls of God's Wrath.

"Then I heard a loud voice from the temple saying to the seven angels, 'Go, pour out the seven bowls of God's wrath on the earth.' The first angel went out and poured out his bowl on the land, and ugly and painful sores broke out on the people who had the mark of the beast and worshiped his image. The second angel poured out his bowl on the sea, and it turned into blood like that of a dead man, and every living thing in the sea died. The third angel poured out his bowl on the rivers and springs of water, and they became blood. Then I heard the angel in charge of the waters say: 'You are just in these judgments, You who are and who were, the Holy One, Because you have so judged; for they have shed the blood of your saints and prophets, and you have given them blood to drink as they deserve.'" "And I heard the altar respond: 'Yes, Lord God Almighty, true and just are Your judgments.'

The fourth angel poured out his bowl on the sun, and the sun was given power to scorch people with fire. They were seared by the intense heat and they cursed the name of God, who had control over these plagues, but they refused to repent and glorify him.

"The fifth angel poured out his bowl on the throne of the beast, and his kingdom was plunged into darkness. Men gnawed their tongues in agony and cursed the God of Heaven because of their pains and their sores, but they refused to repent of what they had done.

"The sixth angel poured out his bowl on the great river Euphrates, and its water was dried up to prepare the way for the kings from the East. Then I saw three evil spirits that looked like frogs; they came out of the mouth of the dragon, and out of the mouth of the beast and out of the mouth of the false prophet. They are spirits of demons performing miraculous signs, and they go out to the kings of the whole world, to gather them for the battle on the great day of God Almighty. "Behold I come like a thief! Blessed is he who stays awake and keeps his clothes with him, so that he may not go naked and be shamefully exposed. Then they gathered the kings together to the place that in Hebrew is called Armageddon. The seventh angel poured out his bowl into the air, and out of the temple came a loud voice from the throne, saying, 'It is done!' Then there came flashes of lightning, rumblings, peals of thunder and a severe earthquake. No earthquake like it has ever occurred since man has been on earth, so tremendous was the quake. The great city split into three parts, and the cities of the nations collapsed.

"God remembered Babylon the Great and gave her the cup filled with the wine of the fury of his wrath. Every island fled away and the mountains could not be found. From the sky huge hailstones of about a hundred pounds each fell upon men. And they cursed God on account of the plague of hail, because the plague was so terrible.

"I have begun. Yes I have begun. The time has come. See I will come on a white horse holding the victory that has fulfilled all that is written in My Word. I speak to My children and I say to you: prepare for My coming for you do not know the day or the hour as I will come as a thief in the night.

"All who call upon My Name will be saved. I say to those who know Me not, come now while there is still time. I say to those who have backslidden, repent while there is still time. I call all on earth to hear My Words for they are true and faithful. Shirley, go to 1 Thessalonians 5:1 – 24,

"Now, brothers, about times and dates we do not need to write to you, for you know very well that the Day of the Lord will come like a thief in the night. While people are saying, 'Peace and safety,' destruction will come on them suddenly, as labor pains on a pregnant woman, and they will not escape. But you, brothers, are not in darkness so that this day should surprise you like a thief. You are all sons of the light and sons of the day. We do not belong to the night or to the darkness. So then, let us not be like the others, who are asleep, but let us be alert and self-controlled.

"For those who sleep, sleep at night, and those who get drunk, get drunk at night. But since we belong to the day, let us be self-controlled, putting on faith, and love as a breastplate and the hope of salvation as a helmet. For God did not appoint us to suffer wrath but to receive salvation through our Lord Jesus Christ.

"He died for us so that, whether we are awake or asleep, we may live together with him. Therefore encourage one another and build each other up, just as in fact you are doing. Now we ask you, brothers, to respect those who work hard among you, who are over you in the Lord and who admonish you. Hold them in the highest regard in love because of their work. Live in peace with each other.

And we urge you, brothers, warn those who are idle, encourage the timid, help the weak, be patient with everyone. Make sure that nobody pays back wrong for wrong, but always try to be kind to each other and to everyone else. "Be joyful always, pray continually; give thanks in all circumstances, for this is God's will for you in Christ Jesus. Do not put out the Spirit's fire; do not treat prophecies with contempt. Test everything. Hold on to the good. Avoid every kind of evil.

May God himself, the God of peace, sanctify you through and through. May your whole spirit, soul and body be kept blameless at the coming of our Lord Jesus Christ. The one who calls you is faithful and he will do it.

"Shirley, this day comes and nothing will stop it for it is written and as it is written so it will be." Yes Lord, it will be as you have said it. S*hirley, go to Revelation 3: 21,* To the Church of Laodicea

"To him who overcomes I will give the right to sit with me on my throne, just as I overcame and sat down with my father on his throne."

"Now I want you to Listen carefully as I say this: I have seen the games people play with Me. They say; 'I love the Lord,' they say; 'I worship the Lord,' and they say, 'I praise the Lord.' But they lie only to themselves for they continue life without Me. I am not blind. I see what they do. Do they think I am blind? I say to those who lie to themselves and to others—know this; I see your lies as I am not blind like you are. I am coming soon for those who are true to Me in all their heart, their mind and their soul.

"They say: 'I am saved,' and 'I am born-again,' but they do not Listen to My Words. Do they not know that I am holy and that I come for a holy people. I see the hearts of men. I see the hidden sin. Do not be fooled for I am God and I am not fooled. I see the shepherds—many do not even come to Me. Many have hidden sin. Many lead My sheep astray. Many have turned away from Me. Many live only to count the sheep. Shepherds, Listen to My Words for I say to you; repent and go after the lost sheep. Some shepherds gather only what it is they want. They eat well and dress in fine clothes while their sheep go without. They have lost their first love. They have set Me aside. I speak now to the Elders of the churches. I see you too. Do you not know that you will be held accountable for the sheep? Do you show the sheep respect? Do you have a kind heart? Do you feed the sheep with a good heart? I want to say to you—be careful for you will be accountable for much if you do not lead by example."

*"I say to the church—repent—pastors, teachers, prophets, elders— **turn to the Gospel and teach what the Gospel teaches! Turn away from your own words.** There is only one Gospel and that is the truth. **Return** to the truth. **Teach** the truth. **Live** the truth. Teach that I come soon. Teach that all **sin leads to death and hell. Teach true repentance and forgiveness. Teach Holiness!** Teach that I come to take only those that have oil in their lamps. The dry lamps—those are the ones that do not hold fast to the truth of the Gospel of Christ.(Bold,added for emphasis).*

"I am Christ, and I am coming for the Body of Christ. Teach that participation with the world is alien to the child of God. Teach that you are in the world but not of the world! I say to the church—teach true salvation and teach that sin leads to death. Return to your foundation, the foundation that the truth teaches. Be true shepherds of the sheep. A true shepherd lays his life down for the sheep. Come, do this now for it is late. Go to Revelation 3:14 – 18,"

To the Church in Laodicea.

"These are the words of the Amen, the faithful and true witness, the ruler of God's creation. I know your deeds, that you are neither cold nor hot. I wish you were either one or the other! So, because you are lukewarm—neither hot nor cold—I am about to spit you out of my mouth. You say, 'I am rich; I have acquired wealth and do not need a thing.' But you do not realize that you are wretched, pitiful, poor, blind and naked. I counsel you to buy from me gold refined in the fire, so you can become rich; and white clothes to wear, so you can cover your shameful nakedness; and salve to put on your eyes, so you can see."

"Shirley, I come that you may write what it is that I say to the churches." Yes Lord. *"Do not fear."* Yes Lord. *"Now Shirley, write down exactly what I tell you."* Yes Lord.

"This is what I say to the world—the One who stands ready will come to judge you. I am the Righteous Judge and there is none other. I came to give My servant My Word that you may hear. Your destiny is in My hand. Shirley go to Revelation 17:1 – 18,"

The Woman and the Beast

"One of the seven angels who had the seven bowls came and said to me, 'Come I will show you the punishment of the great prostitute, who sits on many waters. With her the kings of the earth committed adultery and the inhabitants of the earth were intoxicated with the wine of her adulteries.' Then the angel carried me away in the Spirit into a desert. There I saw a woman sitting on a scarlet beast that was covered with blasphemous names and had seven heads and ten horns. The woman was dressed in purple and scarlet, and was glittering with gold, precious stones and pearls. She held a golden cup in her hand, filled with abominable things and filth of her adulteries. This title was written on her forehead:

MYSTERY, BABYLON THE GREAT, THE MOTHER OF PROSTITUTES AND OF THE ABOMINATIONS OF THE EARTH.

"I saw that the woman was drunk with the blood of the saints, the blood of those who bore testimony to Jesus. When I saw her, I was greatly astonished. Then the angel said to me: 'Why are you astonished? I will tell explain to you the mystery of the woman and of the beast she rides, which has the seven heads and ten horns.

The beast, which you saw, once was, now is not, and will come up out of the Abyss and go to his destruction. The inhabitants of the earth whose names have not been written in the book of life from the creation of the world will be astonished when they see the beast, because he once was, now is not, and yet will come. "This calls for a mind with wisdom. The seven heads are seven hills on which the woman sits. They are also seven kings. Five have fallen, one is, the other has not yet come: but when he does come, he must remain for a little while. The beast who once was, and now is not, is an eighth king. He belongs to the seven and is going to his destruction. The ten horns you saw are ten kings who have not yet received a kingdom, but who for one hour will receive authority as kings along with the beast. They have one purpose and will give their power and authority to the beast. They will make war against the Lamb, but the Lamb will overcome them because he is Lord of lords and King of kings—and with him will be his called, chosen and faithful followers.

"Then the angel said to me, 'The waters you saw, where the prostitute sits, are peoples, multitudes, nations and languages. The beast and the ten horns you saw, will hate the prostitute, they will bring her to ruin and leave her naked; they will eat her flesh and burn her with fire. "For God will put it into their hearts to accomplish his purpose by agreeing to give the beast their power to rule, until God's words are fulfilled. The woman you saw is the great city that rules over the kings of the earth.'"

Saturday, 3 March, 2012, Time: 10:21 a.m.

"Shirley, know this. The world stands ready to fulfill My written Word. It is on the precipice of falling as it has reached its height. I come to warn people of this world, to surrender to Me before this dreadful day comes. It is the day the Lord God Almighty has made and the gates of hell will not prevail over it.

"This is the day spoken of many times in the Bible and it is now coming to its fulfillment very soon. I call on the people of this world, come now to the Lord God Almighty and come out of Babylon and its filthy den. It is filled with all kinds of demons and is the mother of harlots who have gone into the world infiltrating the very essence of spirituality.

"I call on you now to come out of her while there still is time. Become wise in what you believe. Seek the only Living God, the Creator of Heaven and Earth. Let My Words resound in your ears and bring sense into your mind that you may search for Me and find Me with your whole heart. I am found, just call on My name and I will hear. Seek Me while you still have time for time is short. I come soon. Those who have ears, hear what I am saying to the

world for it will come upon you when you least expect it. Do not be foolish and do not be arrogant for it will end in death, eternal death.

"I call you out of the kingdom of darkness into My Kingdom of Light and everlasting life. Come now so that you may be saved. Whoever calls on My Name will be saved, that is My Word and I fulfill My Word—it is never returned void. I am that I am. Jesus Christ who came and laid his life down for you so that your sins will not be held against you unless you deny Me. Seek Me now while there is time. This is what I say to the world, seek Me and come out of her now! Come now Shirley, let us go forward." Yes Lord. I sense the Lord's determination. *"Go to Revelation 7: 9 & 10,"*

"After this I looked and there before me was a great multitude that no one could count, from every nation, tribe, people and language, standing before the throne and in front of the Lamb. They were wearing white robes and were holding palm branches in their hands. And they cried out in a loud voice: 'Salvation belongs to our God, who sits on the Throne, and to the Lamb.'"

"Now Listen carefully." Yes Lord. *"See I have white robes waiting for each one that will come and surrender his heart to Me. You will receive this because you did not deny Me or My Father in heaven. Heaven waits in anticipation for this day to welcome you into the place God has prepared for you. Come and be washed by My blood and be whiter than snow. Come now so that you may inherit your reward."*

This is beautiful Lord and it is exciting. I am so happy for those who will hear You Lord. *"Yes Shirley and I have much waiting for those who will come."* Thank you Lord. *"Shirley, we are going to change again and this will be different. So Listen carefully."* Yes Lord. *"Go to Revelation 18: 1 – 24,*

The Fall of Babylon

"After this I saw another angel coming down from heaven. He had great authority, and the earth was illuminated by his splendor. With a mighty voice he shouted: 'Fallen! Fallen is Babylon the Great!

She has become a home for demons and a haunt for every evil spirit, a haunt for every unclean and detestable bird. For all the nations have drunk the maddening wine of her adulteries. The kings of the earth committed adultery with her, and the merchants of the earth grew rich from her excessive luxuries.

"Then I heard another voice from heaven say: 'Come out of her, my people, so that you will not share in her sins, so that you will not receive any of her plagues; for her sins are piled up to heaven, and God has remembered her crimes. Give back to her as she has given; pay her back double for what she has done. Mix her a double portion from her own cup. Give her as much torture and grief as the glory and luxury she gave herself. In her heart she boasts, 'I sit as queen; I am not a widow, and I will never mourn.' Therefore in one day her plagues will overtake her: death, mourning and famine. She will be consumed by fire, for mighty is the Lord God who judges her.

"When the kings of the earth who committed adultery with her and shared her luxury see the smoke of her burning they will weep and mourn over her. Terrified at her torment, they will stand far off and cry: 'Woe! Woe, O great city, O Babylon, city of power! In one hour your doom has come!'

"The merchants of the earth will weep and mourn over her because no one buys their cargoes any more—cargoes of gold, silver, precious stones and pearls; fine linen, purple, silk and scarlet cloth; every sort of citron wood, and articles of every kind made of ivory, costly wood, bronze, iron and marble; cargoes of cinnamon and spice, of incense, myrrh and frankincense, of wine and olive oil, of fine flour and wheat; cattle and sheep; horses and carriages; and bodies and souls of men.

"They will say, the fruit you longed for is gone from you. All your riches and splendor have vanished, never to be recovered. The merchants who sold these things and gained their wealth from her will stand far off, terrified at her torment. They will weep and mourn and cry out: 'Woe! Woe, O great city, dressed in fine linen, purple and scarlet, and glittering with gold, precious stones and pearls! In one hour such great wealth has been brought to ruin!'

"Every sea captain, and all who travel by ship, the sailors, and all who earn their living from the sea, will stand far off. When they see the smoke of her burning, they will exclaim, 'Was there ever a city like this great city?' They will throw dust on their heads, and with weeping and mourning cry out:

"Woe! Woe, O great city, where all who had ships on the sea
became rich through her wealth! In one hour she has been brought to ruin! Rejoice over her, O heaven! Rejoice, saints and apostles and prophets! God has judged her for the way she treated you.

"Then a mighty angel picked up a boulder the size of a large millstone and threw it into the sea, and said: 'With such violence the great city of Babylon will be thrown down, never to be found again, the music of harpists and musicians, flute players and trumpeters will never be heard in you again. No workman of any trade will ever be found in you again. The sound of a millstone will never be heard in you again. The light of a lamp will never shine in you again. The voice of bridegroom and bride will never be heard in you again. "Your merchants were the world's great men. By your magic spell all the nations were led astray. In her was found the blood of prophets and of the saints, and of all who have been killed on earth."

Time: 1:55 p.m.

"Listen now for I have this to say to those who will hear." Yes Lord. *"To those who will hear: We have begun this book together and I have brought you to the place in understanding that time is short. Now I want you to understand that many things will occur on earth that you will not see coming. Satan is preparing to bring his power to its fulfilment in the world. He will direct himself right into your home. You will not understand it nor see it coming but I will tell you."*

Sunday, 4 March, 2012, Time: 7:41 p.m.

"Listen carefully." Yes, Lord. *"Go to Revelation 12,* The Woman and the Dragon,

"A great and wondrous sign appeared in heaven: a woman clothed with the sun, with the moon under her feet and a crown of twelve stars on her head. She was pregnant and cried out in pain as she was about to give birth. Then another sign appeared in heaven: an enormous red dragon with seven heads and ten horns and seven crowns on his heads. His tail swept a third of the stars out of the sky and flung them to the earth. The dragon stood in front of the woman who was about to give birth, so that he might devour her child the moment it was born.

"She gave birth to a son, a male child, who will rule all the nations with an iron scepter. And her child was snatched up to God and to his throne. The woman fled into the desert to a place prepared for her by God, where she might be taken care of for 1,260 days. And there was war in heaven, Michael and his angels fought against the dragon, and the dragon and his angels fought back. But he was not strong enough, and they lost their place in heaven. The great dragon was hurled down – that ancient serpent called the devil, or Satan, who leads the whole world astray. He was hurled to the Earth, and his angels with him. Then I heard a loud voice in heaven say:
'Now have come the salvation
And the power and the kingdom of our god,
And the authority of his Christ.
For the accuser of our brothers,
Who accuses them before our God day and night,
Has been hurled down.
They overcame him
By the blood of the Lamb
And by the word of their testimony,
They did not love their lives so much
As to shrink from death.
Therefore rejoice, you heavens and you who dwell in them!
But woe to the earth and the sea,
Because the devil has gone down to you!
He is filled with fury because he knows that his time is short.'

"When the dragon saw that he had been hurled to the earth, he pursued the woman who had given birth to the male child. The woman was given the two wings of a great eagle, so that she might fly to the place prepared for her in the desert, where she would be taken care of for a time, times and half a time, out of the serpent's reach. Then from his mouth the serpent spewed water like a river, to overtake the woman and sweep her away with the torrent. But the earth helped the woman by opening its mouth and swallowing the river that the dragon had spewed out of his mouth.

Then the dragon was enraged at the woman and went off to make war against the rest of her offspring – those who obey God's commandments and hold to the testimony of Jesus."

Monday, 5 March, 2012, Time: 11: 00 a.m.

"Shirley, fear nothing for I am with you." Thank you, Lord.
"Shirley, write this down carefully." Yes, Lord. *"I, Jesus, say to all those that will listen: A time of great tribulation is coming upon the earth. I speak about the end times to those who will hear My Words. Satan is let out and is coming to take what he has prepared. He is*

coming to also take revenge on those who are Mine. He is coming and is come to bring the world against Me. I say to those who will listen—be prepared for he will come in power. This power as has yet not been seen. It will come in torrents and will be severe and the world will follow him and the world will trust him. Only My own will see. These are those that he will pursue with great force. He will pursue many and he will kill many. These are the saints of the tribulation. These are the saints that heaven awaits. This is what the Lord Jesus says to those who will hear. The time is here and it is about to be as it is written."

Time: 2:05 p.m.

"Shirley, write this down clearly." Yes, Lord.
"I have begun with this Word to you, so that you may be warned. Those that heed My Word and come to Me will receive Me. Those that remain arrogant will receive that which arrogance brings. I say to My own—know that I am with you and in you. Know that I will come and take all that is Mine. This is what the Lord God Almighty says to those who will listen.

"All the arrogant will become more arrogant. They will scoff at My Word for they are scoffers of God. But do they not understand that arrogance is ignorance. Yes, many are well educated and hold positions in this world and are respected by those around them, but God is not a respecter of man's abilities.

"I am a respecter of humbleness because with humbleness comes respect for each other. Arrogance respects no one but only itself. Yes, arrogance is ignorance. The ignorance I talk about is ignorance for what is plainly seen by My Creation. My Creation is the proof of My Word. My Word is the proof of My Creation. Yes ignorance of Me is what I say. Do you not know that I use the simple things in life to confuse the wise.

"My Word is simple but your arrogance reveals your ignorance. You, that scoff at Me and scoff at My Creation and scoff at My Word, you are ignorant. You are without understanding. You are foolish. You have not listened or have not even looked for truth. If you had, you would know that I am the Way, the Truth and the Life. I say to you, come now and become gold refined by fire, for it is here waiting. I say again, all who call on My Name will be saved. Come now while there is still time. I am that I am."

Tuesday, 6 March, 2012, Time: 8:40 a.m.

"Shirley, today you will receive that which you wait for." Yes, Lord. *"Now write down all you receive carefully."* Yes, Lord.
"Go to Isaiah 28:16 – 23,"

"So this is what the Sovereign Lord says: see, I lay a stone in Zion, a tested stone, a precious cornerstone for a sure foundation; the one who trusts will never be dismayed. I will make justice the measuring line and righteousness the plumb line; hail will sweep away your refuge, the lie, and water will overflow your hiding place. Your covenant with death will be annulled; your agreement with the grave will not stand, when the overwhelming scourge sweeps by, you will be beaten down by it. As often as it comes it will carry you away, morning after morning, by day and by night, it will sweep through. The understanding of this message will bring sheer terror. The bed is too short to stretch out on, the blanket too narrow to wrap around you. The Lord will rise up as he did at Mount Perazim, He will rouse himself as in the valley of Gibeon – to do his work, his strange work, and perform his task, his alien task. Now stop your mocking, or your chains will become heavier; the Lord, the Lord Almighty, has told me of the destruction decreed against the whole land. Listen and hear my voice; pay attention and hear what I say."

"Shirley, Listen carefully." Yes Lord. *"All who know Me, know My Word. Come now and let us talk. You have seen the work of My hands, you read My Words. Consider the signs of the time. They continue their lives without realizing that time is short. I have given you My Word and I want you to rouse yourself out of your sleep, stand up and pay attention. I want you to prepare. I want you to understand, I want you to know. I say to you now; open your eyes and hear My Words for they are true and faithful. Come out of your slumber. Rouse yourself and shake off the sleep for now is the time to prepare. Come let us talk. Come and spend time with Me that we may talk. Come for the time is now. Shirley, go to Isaiah 53,"*

"Who has believed our message and to whom has the arm of the Lord been revealed? He grew up before him like a tender shoot, and like a root out of dry ground. He had no beauty or majesty to attract us to him, nothing in his appearance that we should desire him. He was despised and rejected by men, a man of sorrows, and familiar with suffering. Like one from whom men hide their faces
He was despised, and we esteemed him not. Surely he took up our infirmities And carried our sorrows, yet we considered him stricken by God, smitten by him, and afflicted. But he was pierced for our transgressions, He was crushed for our iniquities; the punishment that brought us peace was upon him, and by his wounds we are healed. We all, like sheep, have gone astray, each of us has turned to his own way; and the Lord has laid on him the iniquity of us all. He was oppressed and afflicted, yet he did not open his mouth; He was led like a Lamb to the slaughter, and as a sheep before her shearers is silent, so he did not open his mouth. By oppression and judgment He was taken away. And who can speak of his descendants?

"For he was cut off from the land of the living; for the transgression of my people he was stricken. He was assigned a grave with the wicked, and with the rich in his death, though he had done no violence, nor was any deceit in his mouth. Yet it was the Lord's will to crush him and cause him to suffer, and though the Lord makes his life a guilt offering, he will see his offspring, and prolong his days, and the will of the Lord will prosper in his hand. After the suffering of his soul, he will see the light of life and be satisfied; by his knowledge my righteous servant will justify many, and he will bear their iniquities.

"Therefore I will give him a portion among the great, and he will divide the spoils with the strong, because he poured out his life unto death, and was numbered with the transgressors. For he bore the sin of many, and made intercession for the transgressors."

"Shirley, now Listen carefully." Yes Lord. *"All those that scoff and reject Me; I give notice to you now. My Word is My Word. My Word speaks of My coming and My going and My coming again. This is a notice to all of earth—I come again and I come as a Lion to bring judgment upon this world that has turned away from Me and has denied Me. I came and paid for your sin and brought salvation and eternal life by My blood that was spilt for you. This is what I say to you—know that I come as the Righteous Judge. I come to judge and I come soon. Nothing can stop what has been written neither you nor the gates of hell will prevail against Me for I am the Holy One. I am at the right hand side of My Father and I wait on Him but I say to you—take heed of My Words for I come to judge this world."*

Wednesday, 7 March, 2012, Time: 8:20 a.m.

"Shirley, write down carefully all that I tell you." Yes Lord.
"Go to Romans 9:23 -27,"

"What if he did this to make the riches of his glory known to the objects of his mercy, whom he prepared in advance for glory—even us, whom he also called, not only from the Jews but also from the Gentiles? As he says in Hosea: 'I will call them 'my people' who are not my people; and I will call her 'my loved one' who is not my loved one, and, it will happen that in the very place where it was said to them, 'You are not my people,' they will be called 'sons of the Living God,' Isaiah cries out concerning Israel: 'Though the number of the Israelites be like the sand by the sea, only the remnant will be saved.'"

"Shirley, I say this now: I have seen the many that come against My loved ones and I know their hearts but I say to them 'I have seen you.' So, since I have seen you I know your plans and if I know your plans then I know your actions and since I know your actions then I know My actions. So as I have said, 'I know you.' Do you think that I do not? Yes, the time is coming when My actions will be seen by the whole earth. No one will escape. Even those who say; 'I am safe.' Be warned, that when I come I will bring My judgments upon the whole earth."

Lord, this work will cause a lot of controversy. *"Yes Shirley that is exactly what I want so that they will take My written Word seriously. For too long now My Word has been ignored, so what am I to do?"* Yes Lord, I see you can only bring a warning to those that will listen. *"You have seen correctly."* Yes, thank you Lord.
"Shirley, now go to Romans 11:13 -17,"

"I am talking to you Gentiles. In as much as I am the apostle to the Gentiles, I make much of my ministry in the hope that I may somehow arouse my own people to envy and save some of them. For if their rejection is the reconciliation of the world, what will their acceptance be but, life from the dead? If the part of the dough offered as first fruits is holy, then the whole batch is holy; if the root is holy, so are the branches. If some of the branches have been broken off, and you, though a wild olive shoot, have been grafted in among the others and now share in the nourishing sap from the olive root." *"Now go to Romans 16:17 & 18,"*

"I urge you, brothers, to watch out for those who cause divisions and put obstacles in your way that are contrary to the teaching you have learned. Keep away from them. For such people are not serving our Lord Christ, but their own appetites. By smooth talk and flattery they deceive the minds of naïve people."

"Shirley, I want My people to know My Word and My soon return but I also want those who do not know Me to find Me through this work." Yes Lord, I pray that they will. *"Shirley, now let us continue: Go to Revelation 11,"* The Two Witnesses.

"I was given a reed like a measuring rod and was told, 'Go and measure the temple of God and the altar, and count the worshipers there. But exclude the outer court, do not measure it, because it has been given to the Gentiles. They will trample on the holy city for 42 months. And I will give power to my two witnesses, and they will prophesy for 1,260 days, clothed in sackcloth.'

"These are the two olive trees and the two lampstands that stand before the Lord of the earth. If anyone tries to harm them, fire comes from their mouths and devours their enemies. This is how anyone who wants to harm them must die. These men have power to shut up the sky so that it will not rain during the time they are prophesying; and they have power to turn the waters into blood and to strike the earth with every kind of plague as often as they want. "Now when they have finished their testimony, the beast that comes up from the Abyss will attack them and overpower and kill them. Their bodies will lie in the street of the great city, which is figuratively called Sodom and Egypt, where also their Lord was crucified. For three and a half days men from every people, tribe, language and nation will gaze on their bodies and refuse them burial.

"The inhabitants of the earth will gloat over them and will celebrate by sending each other gifts, because these two prophets had tormented those who live on the earth. But after the three and a half days a breath of life from God entered them, and they stood on their feet, and terror struck those who saw them. Then they heard a loud voice from heaven saying to them, 'Come up here.' And they went up to heaven in a cloud, while their enemies looked on.

"At that very hour there was a severe earthquake and a tenth of the city collapsed. Seven thousand people were killed in the earthquake, and the survivors were terrified and gave glory to the God of heaven. The second woe has passed; the third woe is coming soon.

"Shirley listen carefully as I tell you." Yes Lord. *"All those that did not accept the Lord will be given these prophets that will come in power and prophecy into the city. They will bring the Word of the Lord Jesus Christ to the world as a final warning of that which will come. It is done so that no one is without excuse."*

Lord, so the people of the earth will see this on their televisions. *"Yes Shirley, they will bring a final warning so that the world will be without excuse."* Yes Lord I understand. *"Shirley, go to Romans 1:2-6,"*

The Gospel of God

"The gospel he promised beforehand through his prophets in the Holy Scriptures regarding his Son, who as to his human nature was a descendant of David, and who through the Spirit of Holiness was declared with power to be the Son of God by his resurrection from the dead: Jesus Christ our Lord. Through him and for his name's sake, we received grace and apostleship to call people from among all the Gentiles to the obedience that comes from faith. And you also are among those who are called to belong to Jesus Christ."

"See, I call you now, as I did then, come and come now for soon comes the time of great tribulation that will fall upon this earth. Come now while grace abounds. Shirley, go to Psalm 114,"

"When Israel came out of Egypt, the house of Jacob from a people of foreign tongue, Judah became God's sanctuary, Israel his dominion. The sea looked and fled, the Jordan turned back; the mountains skipped like rams, the hills like lambs, Why was it, O sea that you fled, O Jordan, that you turned back, you mountains, that you skipped like rams, you hills, like lambs? Tremble, O earth, at the presence of the Lord, at the presence of the God of Jacob, who turned the rock into a pool, the hard rock into springs of water."

Thursday, 8 March, 2012
Funeral: A farewell to a most humble man in Christ who went to be with the Lord.

Friday, 9 March, 2012, Time: 9:00 a.m.

"Shirley, write this down carefully." Yes Lord.
"Go to Romans 2:1 – 16; God's Righteous Judgment

"You, therefore, have no excuse, you who pass judgment on someone else, for at whatever point you judge the other, you are condemning yourself, because you who pass judgment do the same things. Now we know that God's judgment against those who do such things is based on truth. So when you, a mere man, pass judgment on them and yet do the same things, do you think you will escape God's judgment? Or do you show contempt for the riches of his kindness, tolerance and patience, not realizing that God's kindness leads you towards repentance.

"But because of your stubbornness and your unrepentant heart, you are storing up wrath against yourself for the day of God's wrath, when his righteous judgment will be revealed. God will give to each person according to what he has done. To those who by persistence in doing good seek glory, honor and immortality, he will give eternal life. But for those who are self-seeking and who reject the truth and follow evil, there will be wrath and anger. There will be trouble and distress for every human being who does evil: first for the Jew, then for the Gentile; but glory, honor and peace for everyone who does good: first for the Jew, then for the Gentile. For God does not show favoritism.

"All who sin apart from the law will also perish apart from the law, and all who sin under the law will be judged by the law. For it is not those who hear the law who are righteous in God's sight, but it is those who obey the law who will be declared righteous. (Indeed, when Gentiles, who do not have the law, do by nature things required by the law, they are a law for themselves, even though they do not have the law, since they show that the requirements of the law are written on their hearts, their consciences also bearing witness, and their thoughts now accusing, now even defending them.) This will take place on the day when God will judge men's secrets through Jesus Christ, as my gospel declares."

"Shirley, all who call on My Name will be saved. All who do not call on My Name will suffer the wrath of God for My Name is above all names and My Word is above all Word. Every knee will bow and every tongue will confess that Jesus Christ is Lord." Yes Lord. Nothing is hidden from God. All is visible by the light of God. *"Those who live in darkness think the dark hides their sin. No, the light of God reveals all sin. I call on those who do not know Me, come now while mercy and grace abound." "Go to 1 Peter 4:1 – 7,"*

"Therefore, since Christ suffered in his body, arm yourselves also with the same attitude, because he who has suffered in his body is done with sin. As a result, he does not live the rest of his earthly life for evil human desires, but rather for the will of God. For you have spent enough time in the past doing what pagans choose to do—living in debauchery, lust, drunkenness, orgies, carousing and detestable idolatry.

"They think it strange that you do not plunge with them into the same flood of dissipation, and heap abuse on you. But they will have to give account to him who is ready to judge the living and the dead. For this is the reason the gospel was preached even to those who are now dead, so that they might be judged according to men in regard to the body, but live according to God in regard to the Spirit. The end of all things is near. Therefore be clear minded and self-controlled so that you can pray.

"Go to 1 Peter: 4:17 & 18,"

"For it is time for judgment to begin with the family of God; and if it begins with us, what will the outcome be for those who do not obey the gospel of God? And, 'If it is hard for the righteous to be saved, what will become of the ungodly and the sinner?'"

"Go to Psalm 21: 8 – 12,"

"Your hand will lay hold on all your enemies; your right hand will seize your foes. At the time of your appearing you will make them like a fiery furnace. In his wrath the Lord will swallow them up, And his fire will consume them. You will destroy their descendants from the earth, their posterity from mankind. Though they plot evil against you and devise wicked schemes, they cannot succeed; for you will make them turn their backs when you aim at them with drawn bow."

"Shirley, I say this to those that will hear; come now before the God Almighty and repent for your ways for they will lead you into the wrath of God. Come now and repent for I call each and every one—come now in earnest prayer and bow before your God in repentance, for **now** *is the time. Come while mercy and grace abound. Shirley, I call all those who will hear and listen to what I am saying to the world for the time for repentance is now. I say to them—let go of your stubbornness and your pride—for the time is now. Come and open the door to your heart and let Me in so that we may meet. Come while grace abounds."*

Lord, you are so patient. *"Yes Shirley, for the time is soon and the number of Gentiles is soon to be fulfilled. I have waited for this day just as heaven awaits this day. I call those who are to come in, to come now while there is still time."* Yes, Lord. *"Go to 1 Peter 3:16 – 22,"*

"Keeping a clear conscience, so that those who speak maliciously against your good behavior in Christ, may be ashamed of their slander. It is better, if it is God's will, to suffer for doing good than, for doing evil. For Christ died for sins once for all, the Righteous for the unrighteous, to bring you to God. He was put to death in body but made alive by the Spirit, through whom also he went and preached to the spirits in prison who disobeyed long ago when God waited patiently in the days of Noah while the ark was being built.
In it only a few people, eight in all, were saved through water, and this water symbolizes baptism that now saves you also—not the removal of dirt from the body but the pledge of a good conscience toward God. It saves you by the resurrection of Jesus Christ, who has gone

into heaven and is at God's right hand—with angels, authorities and powers in submission to him.

"Go to John 3:16,"

Jesus speaking:

"For God so loved the world that he gave his One and only Son, that whosoever believes in him shall not perish but have eternal life."

Lord, this is the most loved and known scripture in the world. *"Yes and it shows the heart of My Father. He loves His creation so much that He gave His only Son. Shirley, the world has been given time to come to reach its fullness of sin. This is written and what is written will come to pass."* Yes, Lord.

"Shirley, go to John 5: 20 – 30,"

Jesus speaking:

"For the father loves the Son and shows him all he does. Yes, to your amazement he will show him even greater things than these. For just as the Father raises the dead and gives them life, even so the Son gives life to whom he is pleased to give it. "Moreover, the Father judges no one, but has entrusted all judgment to the Son that all may honor the Son just as they honor the Father. He who does not honor the Son does not honor the Father, who sent him.

"I tell you the truth, whoever hears my word and believes him who sent me has eternal life and will not be condemned; he as crossed over from death to life. I tell you the truth, a time is coming and has now come when the dead will hear the voice of the Son of God and those who hear will live."For as the father has life in himself, so he has granted the Son to have life in himself. And he has given him authority to judge because he is the Son of Man. Do not be amazed at this, for a time is coming when all who are in their graves will hear his voice and come out—those who have done good will rise to live, and those who have done evil will rise to be condemned. By myself I can do nothing, I judge only as I hear, and my judgment is just, for I seek not to please myself but him who sent me."

Yes Lord, all power and authority is given to You. *"Yes, Shirley and that is why every knee will bow and every tongue will confess that Jesus Christ is Lord."* Yes Lord that is exactly what you mean!

Saturday, 10 March, 2012, Time: 9:00 a.m.

"Shirley, listen carefully now." Yes Lord.
"Be still and know that I am God." Yes Lord.
"All those that live their lives according to their ways will not receive anything from Me. I am the Lord God Almighty and I am the One that can save or destroy. I call on all those that will hear what the Lord is saying to the church today. Surrender your lives to Me. Let Me lead you. Take your hands off the steering wheel. Come to Me and let Me lead the way, for I am your High Priest. Come and follow Me."

"Shirley, now go to Matthew 8:18 – 22,"

The Cost of Following Jesus:

"When Jesus saw the crowd around him, he gave orders to cross to the other side of the lake. Then a teacher of the law came to him and said, 'Teacher, I will follow you wherever you go.' Jesus replied, 'Foxes have holes and the birds of the air have nests, but the Son of Man has no place to lay his head.' Another disciple said to him, 'Lord first let me go and bury my father.' But Jesus told him, 'Follow me, and let the dead bury their own dead.'"

"Shirley, many have come to Me but do not truly surrender their lives. They continue to make the wrong decisions that affect their lives. If only they would surrender their lives to Me so that they may hear My voice and follow Me. I am the way, the life and the truth. I say to all— come now to Me and hear My voice that I may lead you. If you follow Me, My way for you will be the truth." Go to Psalm 26:1 – 3,"

"Vindicate me, O Lord, for I have led a blameless life; I have trusted in the Lord without wavering. Test me, O Lord, and try me, examine my heart and my mind; for your love is ever before me, and I walk continually in your truth."

Lord, David walked in your truth and with an open heart. *"Yes Shirley and this is available to all that will truly surrender their lives to Me. Shirley many do not walk with Me. Many do not know My voice and I say again, My sheep know My voice. To know Me is to love Me and to obey Me."* Yes, Lord.

"Go to Matthew 7:13 & 14,"

Jesus speaking:

"Enter through the narrow gate. For wide is the gate and broad is the road that leads to destruction, and many enter through it. But small is the gate and narrow the road that leads to life, and only a few find it."

"Go to Matthew 7:22 & 23,"

"Many will say to me on that day, 'Lord, Lord, did we not prophesy in your name, and in your name drive out demons and perform many miracles?' Then I will tell them plainly, 'I never knew you. Away from me, you evildoers!'"

"Go to Matthew 7:24 -27,"

Jesus speaking:

"Therefore everyone who hears these words of mine and puts them into practice is like a wise man who built his house on the rock. The rain came down, the streams rose, and the winds blew and beat against that house; yet it did not fall, because it had its foundation on the rock. But everyone who hears these words of mine and does not put them into practice is like a foolish man who built his house on sand. The rain came down, the streams rose, and the winds blew and beat against that house and it fell with a great crash."

"See Shirley, My Word is the same yesterday, today and forever. My Word is never returned void. Yes, many say they are saved when they enter the narrow road but that is only the beginning. The narrow road, is the road of life in Me. I am the life." Yes, Lord. Lord many believe that 'once saved always saved.' *"Shirley, accepting Me into their heart must come with love for Me and I say again, to love Me is to obey Me. I am the Way. I am the Way into heaven."* Yes, Lord, this is true. *"Therefore, I am the Way, the Truth and the Life. No one comes to the Father but by Me."*

Lord I understand that when one is saved, this is the beginning of the walk with You. Lord You say in your Word: small is the gate and NARROW is the road that leads to life and only a FEW find it. Lord then we must obey You and follow You according to what Your Word has taught us. Lord so our journey of life in You only begins when we accept You as our Lord and Savior?

"Yes Shirley, many in the church believe they are saved, but they do not obey Me. They live their lives according to their will." Yes, Lord. Lord so 'once saved, always saved' is not the truth? *"No Shirley, that is why many will be disappointed when I will say to them; 'Away from Me, you evil doers.'"* Lord, many have been taught incorrectly. *"Yes, Shirley, they have false teachers. My Word has been torn apart by those who want their ears tickled."* Yes, Lord, I understand. *"Shirley, once you enter the narrow road, it is the path to holiness. I am holy and My sheep must pursue holiness. Their lives must change and will change in pursuit of holiness. I come for My bride that is spotless and blameless."* Yes, Lord.

"Go to Matthew 7:15,"

Jesus speaking:

"Watch out for false prophets, they come to you in sheep's clothing, but inwardly they are ferocious wolves."

Lord, this will cause a lot of controversy. *"Yes Shirley, but the truth remains the truth. That is why each one must work out salvation in fear and trembling. Eternal life is a free gift to all those that accept it with their hearts and turn away from sin to lead a life in Me. I am Holy and My own know My voice and must work out their lives in fear and trembling."* Yes, Lord, I understand. *"I bought their lives with My life. I paid the price of sin. It is a free gift to all that will heed My Word."* Yes, Lord. *"My blood was poured out for those who accept this free gift that washes away all sin and all guilt. By My stripes you are healed."*

Yes, Lord, I understand and I pray that many will hear and understand the price You paid. I also know Lord that I have fallen short at times. *"Yes, Shirley that is why I said earlier that to walk this path it must be done in forgiveness. You forgive others as I forgive you. The narrow path is a spiritual journey of growth in Me."*

Lord, let Me understand this clearly—it begins with salvation and obedience in the Word, within a relationship with You providing we walk in forgiveness. So we must repent of even our tiny sins. This will bring us to a level of holiness that will conclude in eternal life. I see Lord so salvation is only the beginning of our spiritual journey. Thank you Lord. *"Shirley, go to Psalm 93: 5,"*

"Your statutes stand firm; holiness adorns your house for

endless days, O Lord."

Lord, I think this is going to make a lot of Christians rethink their journey with You. *"Shirley, this is My Word to them: those that hear this and change their lives and live according to My Word, will receive their rewards. This is My call to those that will Listen. Come now, come while grace abounds. Shirley, go to Revelation 3:7 – 13,"*

To the Church of Philadelphia:

"These are the words of him who is holy and true, who holds the key of David. What he opens no one can shut, and what he shuts no one can open. I know your deeds. See, I have placed before you an open door that no one can shut. I know that you have little strength, yet you have kept my word and have not denied my name. I will make those who are of the synagogue of Satan, who claim to be Jews though they are not, but are liars – I will make them come and fall down at your feet and acknowledge that I have loved you. Since you have kept my command to endure patiently, I will also keep you from the hour of trial that is going to come upon the whole world to test those who live on the earth.

"I am coming soon. Hold on to what you have, so that no one will take your crown. Him who overcomes I will make a pillar in the temple of my God. Never again will he leave it. I will write on him the name of my God and the name of the city of my God, the new Jerusalem, which is coming down out of heaven from my God; and I will also write on him my new name. He who has an ear, let him hear what the Spirit says to the churches."

"Shirley, go to Romans 4:22 – 25,"

This is why it was credited to him as righteousness. The words 'it was credited to him' were written not for him alone, but also for us, to whom God will credit righteousness—for us who believe in him who raised Jesus our Lord from the dead. He was delivered over to death for our sins and was raised to life for our justification.

"Shirley, this is for all who believe in Me and follow Me, to come to where I am." Yes, Lord and thank you, Lord.

Sunday, 11 March, 2012, Time: 10:40 p.m.

"Shirley, I want you to listen carefully." Yes, Lord.
"I call on all the nations of this earth; I am that I am. I have given you this Word to come to Me while there is still time and while mercy and grace abound. Come now and receive living water."

Go to Isaiah 55:1,"
Invitation to the Thirsty.

"Come, all you who are thirsty, come to the waters; and you who have no money, come, buy and eat! Come buy wine and milk without money and without cost. Why spend money on what is not bread, and your labor on what does not satisfy? Listen, Listen to me, and eat what is good, and your soul will delight in the richest of fare. Give ear and come to me; hear me, that your soul may live.

I will make an everlasting covenant with you, My faithful love promised to David. See, I have made him a witness to the peoples, a leader and commander of the peoples. Surely you will summon nations you know not, and nations that do not know you will hasten to you, because of the Lord your God, the holy one of Israel, for he has endowed you with splendor. "Seek the Lord while he may be found; call on him while he is near.

Let the wicked forsake his way and the evil man his thoughts. Let him turn to the Lord, and he will have mercy on him and to our God, for he will freely pardon. For my thoughts are not your thoughts, neither are your ways my ways, declares the Lord.
As the heavens are higher than the earth, so are my ways higher than your ways and my thoughts than your thoughts. As the rain and the snow come down from heaven, and do not return to it without watering the earth and making it bud and flourish, so that it yields seed for the sower and bread for the eater, so is my word that goes out from my mouth: it will not return to me empty, but will accomplish what I desire and achieve the purpose for which I sent it.

"You will go out in joy and be led forth in peace; the mountains and hills will burst into song before you, and all the trees of the field will clap their hands. Instead of the thorn bush will grow the pine tree, and instead of briers the myrtle will grow. This will be for the Lord's renown, for an everlasting sign which will not be destroyed."

"Shirley, now listen carefully." Yes, Lord. *"All who hear My call and come will receive living water that will drive away the thirst. Come and receive what God Almighty has given to you. Come and cast your burdens upon the Lord and receive what the Lord has given you—a gift of eternal life and salvation for all who call on the Name of the Lord. My call goes out to all the nations of the earth. Listen for the time is **now**. What good is it if a man gains the whole world but loses his soul. Come and buy from Me eternal life. I laid My life down that you may live. I hung on the tree that you may be washed by My blood and cleansed of sin and guilt. Come now as you are and receive what God has given you. Come now while there is still time. Come soon! I want none to perish but all to receive eternal life. Soon comes a time of great trouble upon the earth. Come now!*

Shirley, go to John 15:10 -14,"

Jesus speaking
"If you obey my commands, you will remain in my love, just as I have obeyed my Father's commands and remain in his love. I have told you this so that my joy may be in you and that your joy may be complete. My command is this: love each other as I have loved you. Greater love has no one than this that he lay down his life for his friends. You are my friends if you do what I command."

"See I came and laid down My life for you. If you come and open the door to your heart and invite Me in, I will come in that we may eat. I say to those who know Me—if you love Me you will obey Me. To love Me is to obey Me. Obey My commands that it may go well with you. Live your lives in obedience to Me. Keep your lamps full of oil for you do not know the time or the hour that I come. I come as a thief in the night. Let no one be fooled. My Word is true and faithful."

Lord, so salvation comes with obedience. If we fall into sin and do not repent we will lose our salvation? *"Yes Shirley, obedience brings holiness. Holiness cannot survive without obedience. I am Holy, therefore, My sheep must seek holiness."* Yes Lord. So salvation is only the beginning. *"Yes Shirley, willful sin will lead to the loss of salvation. If you obey My commands you will remain in My love."*

Lord I am so happy that You have made this clear. I know many Christians who are only Christians on Sundays because they do not take their salvation seriously. Lord, You paid the price for our salvation! *"Yes Shirley and to those who do not listen, they will be disappointed."* Yes, Lord, it will be too late.

Monday, 12 March, 2012, Time: 8:45 a.m.

"Shirley, I want you to listen carefully as we go forward." Yes, Lord. *"I come soon and I want all to be saved. Since the beginning I have called on you to come to Me. To come and follow Me for a time is coming when the doors will shut and no one can enter. I have done all for you and now as the time comes for My return I call out to the world and say:*

"This is the day the Lord has made—the day when no one can hide. For it is written and so it will be. Listen, hear My Voice. For I am the Lord God Almighty, the King of kings and the Lord of lords! The Holy One—the Shepherd of the sheep—the Anointed One—the Son of God—the High Priest—the Alpha and the Omega! I am the Beginning and the End no one comes to the Father but by Me!" *"Shirley."* Yes Lord. *"My heart cries out to the arrogant for they know not what they do. I have done all for them but they deny Me."* Yes, Lord, they think that they have the answers for everything. *"Yes, Shirley and yet they are foolish."* Yes, Lord. *"I come with an Iron Scepter to rule. See I come on a white horse in such power, who can stand against Me?"* Yes Lord. *"Will the arrogant Listen?"* Lord they are stubborn.

"Yes Shirley so they will receive all that their arrogance and stubbornness brings. They dishonor My name and swear by their laws. They have forsaken the statutes in the Bible. They bring judgment upon all." Yes Lord they have turned away from You and Your Word. *"Yes Shirley and so it shall be as it is written."* Yes Lord. *"Go to Psalm 14:1-3,"*

"The fool says in his heart, 'There is no God.' They are corrupt, their deeds are vile; there is no one who does good. The Lord looks down from heaven on the sons of men to see if there are any who understand and any who seek God. All have turned aside, they have together become corrupt, there is no one who does good, not even one."

Lord, the world is full of corruption. *"Yes Shirley, they have become a law unto themselves. They have turned away from My law and now they run on a path of destruction."* Yes Lord. *"Go to Revelation 19:11 – 16,"*

The Rider on the White Horse

"I saw heaven standing open and there before me was a white horse, whose rider is called Faithful and True. With justice he judges and makes war. His eyes are like blazing fire, and on his head are many crowns. He has a name written on him that no one knows but he himself. He is dressed in a robe dipped in blood, and his name is the 'Word of God.' "The armies of heaven were following him, riding on white horses and dressed in fine linen, white and clean. Out of his mouth comes a sharp sword with which to strike down the nations. He will rule them with an iron scepter. He treads the winepress of the fury of the wrath of God Almighty. On his robe and on his thigh he has his name.

KING OF KINGS AND LORD OF LORDS."

"Shirley, people think only that I am a God of love." Yes Lord that is very wide spread in the world and Lord they do not understand that You are Holy and Just. *"That is correct, My daughter, they do not understand*!" Lord, some say the Bible is vicious and full of blood and they question and say—'I thought your God is a God of love?' *"Shirley I am a God of love. I gave My life for all."* Yes Lord.

"Shirley, what some fail to see is that they themselves are vicious. I say to them; 'look at your history!' But I also say to those who have no understanding of God; 'God is Holy!' Yes, Lord. *"I come to judge the world and all its sin. Holiness is Justice. I am the Righteous Judge."* Yes, Lord, but they do not understand.

"Shirley, go to Ezekiel 9," Idolaters Killed

"Then I heard him call out in a loud voice, 'Bring the guards of the city here, each with a weapon in his hand.' And I saw six men coming from the direction of the upper gate, which faces north, each with a deadly weapon in his hand. With them was a man clothed in linen who had a writing kit at his side. They came in and stood beside the bronze altar. Now the glory of the God of Israel went up from above the cherubim, where it had been, and moved to the threshold of the temple. Then the Lord called to the man clothed in linen who had the writing kit at his side and said to him, 'Go throughout the city of Jerusalem and put a mark on the foreheads of those who grieve and lament over all the detestable things that are done in it.'

"As I listened, he said to the others, 'Follow him through the city and kill, without showing pity or compassion. Slaughter old men, young men and maidens, women and children, but do not touch anyone who has the mark. Begin at my sanctuary.' So they began with the elders who were in front of the temple. Then he said to them, 'Defile the temple and fill the courts with the slain. Go!' So they went out and began killing throughout the city.

"While they were killing and I was left alone, I fell face down, crying out, 'Ah Sovereign Lord! Are you going to destroy the entire remnant of Israel in this outpouring of your wrath on Jerusalem?' He answered me, 'The sin of the house of Israel and Judah is exceedingly great; the land is full of bloodshed and the city is full of injustice. They say, "The Lord has forsaken the land; the Lord does not see." So I will not look on them with pity or spare them, but I will bring down on their own heads what they have done.' Then the man in linen with the writing kit at his side brought back word, saying, 'I have done as you commanded.'"

"Shirley, do you know why I did this?" Yes, Lord, because in Ezekiel 8 they had turned against You by serving idols and their land was full of bloodshed and their cities were full of injustice. They also said that You cannot see them.

"Know this; I have seen the sin in the world. Lawlessness prevails and corruption has filled the earth." Yes Lord, murder is rife and nation rises against nation. *"Yes Shirley and if I do not return man will continue as all of history has shown."* Yes Lord I understand but Lord,

man does not learn from his history. *"Shirley man is on his own path to destruction."* Yes Lord I can see this and I understand Lord that unless You return man will never stop repeating history until he wipes himself out and destroys the earth. *"Shirley you have seen correctly."* Thank you Lord.

"Shirley, man has turned away from My Word. He has given himself over to a path of destruction. He is blind and does not see his sin." Lord, some say to me, 'But I lead a good life. I obey the rules of the land.' *"Yes, Shirley and that is good, but they still do not live by My rules. They are blind to My rules. You see until they come to Me with a heart that acknowledges sin they remain in sin. They remain blind to their sin. They do not see their lies."*

Lord, they tell me that they do not lie or steal. *"Yes Shirley, that is because they are blind. How can they say they have never lied when I know that they have? See this is the blindness that I speak of."* Yes Lord You have made this very clear. *"Listen carefully."* Yes Lord. *"I am giving over to man, all that he deserves. He has defiled My Name and he has turned away from My Word. He has taken himself and put himself upon My Throne. He has turned to serve other gods and has forsaken My Word. He is arrogant and filled with pride. His own wisdom leads him and he says, 'Who can stop me.' But I say to man, 'Come, now is the time. Come and repent before Me for I am about to bring judgment upon the whole earth. I call you now—come now while mercy and grace abound.'"*

Tuesday, 13 March, 2012, Time: 9:15 a.m.

"Shirley, listen carefully." Yes Lord. *"Go to Psalm 11:2 -7,"*

"For look, the wicked bend their bows; they set their arrows against the strings to shoot from the shadows at the upright in heart.

When the foundations are being destroyed, what can the righteous do? The Lord is in his holy temple; the Lord is on his heavenly throne. He observes the sons of men, his eyes examine them.

The Lord examines the righteous, but the wicked and those who love violence his soul hates. "On the wicked he will rain fiery coals and burning sulphur; a scorching wind will be their lot. For the Lord is righteous, he loves justice, upright men will see his face."

"Now Shirley, write this down Word for Word." Yes, Lord.
"See I come soon to take those who are set aside for Me. They are Mine. But on those who have destroyed the foundations on which I built My church, I will bring judgment and none will escape.

Go to Matthew 7:15 – 20,"

Jesus speaking:

"Watch out for false prophets. They come to you in sheep's clothing, but inwardly they are ferocious wolves. By their fruit you will recognize them. Do people pick grapes from thorn bushes, or figs from thistles? Likewise every good tree bears good fruit, but a bad tree bears bad fruit. A good tree cannot bear bad fruit, and a bad tree cannot bear good fruit. Every tree that does not bear good fruit is cut down and thrown into the fire. Thus, by their fruit you will recognize them."

"I speak to My church now; be careful that you follow the foundations set by Me. I say to you, 'Return to your first love.' Did I not tell you to test the spirits? See how My foundations have been shaken by those who call themselves pastor, prophet, teacher. Yes, I speak to you, those who have turned My church into a business; who have forsaken the poor, widows and orphans. These are those that I asked you to take care of. Yes, you dress in fine clothes and make yourselves rich. Have you done this at the cost of My sheep? Do they have food? Do they have help? No, you enrich yourselves at the price of My sheep. Money, money, money is all you want.

*"You say to the poor, "Give," when they do not have food. How am I supposed to judge this? Yes, you have walked away from My foundation. You have destroyed My Name. But I tell you, unless you **repent and return to My foundation and go and find the lost sheep,** I will have no mercy on you. You who are a disgrace before My eyes. You have scattered My sheep. Many do not come to church anymore because of you. Yes, you are a disgrace in My eyes. I tell you now; repent and go and find My lost sheep those righteous people who have no church to go to.*

"Do you think I cannot see? Do you think I am blind? My righteous children call out to Me all day long crying for the church. But you, in your own glory are blind. Yes, you are the ones that are blind. I say to each one of you, repent and gather My sheep. Come in truth and with a contrite heart before Me. Unless you come you will receive My judgment and I will have no mercy on you. Come now while My mercy and My grace abound." Lord, You are angry. *"Yes Shirley, I now arise and give warning to those that will listen. For those that will not listen, judgment awaits them."* Yes, Lord.
"Shirley, I come to judge first My church and then the world. This is a warning to the church. I came to build the body of the church and gave a sound foundation, so only the righteous will fill My Body.

"I call all those who are of the house of Babylon—come out of her now. Heed My call. Come to the foundation I have set. Leave the churches that are not of Me. I am Jesus Christ. I am your Savior. There is none other. I am the only mediator between God and you. Call on My Name, come and serve Me. Leave behind all that is not of Me. Leave your statues and their rules of the church. I am the Way, the Truth and the Life. There is no other way. Unless you come, you too will be destroyed. Please listen to My call—for now is the time. Come that I may bless you and save you. "I speak to all who say they are a Christian—are you? Do you know Me? Do you know My Word? Am I real to you or just a figment of your imagination? Yes, you who profess to be Christian. I say to you now—are you? I call on you now—come and repent for your sins and follow Me that you may be saved. Do not be foolish for I am not fooled. Come now while mercy and grace abound.

"Shirley, I arise now to judge first My church and then the world. I call on all the leaders of the churches. Take yourselves off My Throne. I am the head of the church not you. Come and bow down before Me that I may forgive you. Many are a disgrace before My eyes. Do not use the authority I have given you to destroy My Name. Repair the foundations and return to your first love. Do this now while grace abounds."

Lord, I pray that they will hear what You are saying to the churches. *"Yes Shirley, I have heard the prayers of the righteous for many, many years, those that have interceded for the churches. Those that have seen their fruits. Those that have seen the foundation shaken. Yes, I have heard all these prayers. I now answer those prayers for they have reached My Father."* Yes, Lord. *"Shirley, Listen carefully now."* Yes, Lord.

"I speak to the world, to those nations that serve My name. Yes I speak to you. You, who have built your nation on My Name! Do you serve Me? Do you protect My Name? Do you defend the rights of My people? Do you honor My Name? You that laid the foundations of your nations on My Name—do you serve Me?" Fear takes hold of me again. I pray and ask the Lord to give me understanding. He answers me.

"I have your heart in My hand. I lead you so much so that you cannot tell the difference." Yes Lord I have these feelings and emotions even although I do not understand them. *"Shirley, you are in Me as I am in you. Therefore, you have My heart and My emotions.* Lord I just want to do what You say and not what I say. I pray that these are all Your Words and not mine. *"Shirley, I know your heart."* Yes, Lord. *"So I say this to you today. Fear nothing for I am in you and with you."* Yes, Lord, thank you. The thought as to whether Isaiah 9 is a prophecy for America came into my mind as I had just read an article about it. The Lord answered my thought.

"Isaiah 9 is for America." Lord, my mind wants to add this and I do not want to do this as the Scriptures must come from You Lord. Please show me? *"Shirley I have given you the heart to hear My heart. That is why you get confused."* Yes, Lord. *"But if you fear, then you will not hear correctly."* Yes, Lord. *"So then, Listen to Me now. Go to Isaiah 9 and add that in. I have given you that Word so that you will understand it."* Thank you Lord. *"Shirley, now go to Isaiah 9: 8 – 21,"*

The Lord's Anger Against Israel:

"The Lord has sent a message against Jacob; it will fall on Israel. All the people will know it—Ephraim and the inhabitants of Samaria—who say with pride and arrogance of heart. The bricks have fallen down, but we will rebuild with dressed stone; the fig trees have been felled, but we will replace them with cedars.

But the Lord has strengthened Rezin's foes against them and has spurred their enemies on. Arameans from the East and Philistines from the West have devoured Israel with open mouth. Yet for all this, his anger is not turned away, His hand is still upraised,

"But the people have not returned to him who struck them, nor have they sought the Lord Almighty. So the Lord will cut off from Israel both head and tail, both palm branch and reed in a single day, the elders and prominent men are the head, the prophets who teach lies are the tail. Those who guide this people mislead them, and those who are guided are led astray. Therefore the Lord will take no pleasure in the young men, nor will he pity the fatherless and widows, for everyone is ungodly and wicked, every mouth speaks vileness. Yet for all this, his anger is not turned away, his hand is still upraised.
"Surely wickedness burns like a fire; it consumes briers and thorns, it sets forest thickets ablaze so that it rolls upward in a column of smoke. By the wrath of the Lord Almighty the land will be scorched and the people will be fuel for the fire; no one will spare his brother.

"On the right they will devour, but still be hungry; on the left they will eat, but not be satisfied. Each will feed on the flesh of his own offspring. Manasseh will feed on Ephraim and Ephraim on Manasseh; together they will turn against Judah. Yet for all this, his anger is not turned away, his hand is still upraised." *"Go to Isaiah 10: 1 – 4,"*

"Woe to those who make unjust laws, to those who issue oppressive decrees, to deprive the poor of their rights and withhold justice from the oppressed of my people, making widows their prey and robbing the fatherless. What will you do on the day of reckoning, when disaster comes from afar? To whom will you run for help? Where will you leave your riches? Nothing will remain but to cringe among the captives or fall among the slain. Yet for all this, his anger is not turned away, his hand is still upraised."

"Now listen carefully." Yes Lord. *"I have raised My hand against those nations that say; 'We are Christian.' They who have turned their backs against Me. They have lost their first love. Money has become their God. They seek Me not. They seek only that which they want. Yes, My upraised hand is against you. You, who have turned your back on My people. You have not kept My Covenant.*
"You, like Israel, have turned away from your God. How then do you think you will survive? You, who have brought in your laws that have replaced My laws. You have forsaken the Lord God Almighty. Yes you have turned against Me. But Listen and Listen well. I give you warning. Unless you repent and return your nation to Me, you will receive all that your arrogance and pride has brought to you. You, who stand in your lofty towers and speak against My Name. You who think you are God. I ask you now—yes leaders, are you Me? You have brought shame upon your nation. You have brought judgment against your nation. Yes, you have gathered around teachers of the Word and prophets who say they are from Me but are not. Yes you have gathered them around you to tickle your ears. You, who call yourselves 'Christians,' you are a disgrace before My eyes. But know this—your judgment awaits you. Do not think that you will escape My judgments!"

Lord, these nations have made the same mistake as Israel did when they stopped worshiping you and it cost them dearly. *"Yes Shirley, they are taking the same road. You have seen correctly."* Thank you Lord. *"This is what the Lord God Almighty says to the nations— repent while there is still time. Repent and turn back to your God before the great and terrible day. Let this be a warning to you. Repent now while mercy and grace abound."* *"Shirley, go to Isaiah 24:1 -6,*

The LORD'S Devastation of the Earth.

"See, the Lord is going to lay waste the earth and devastate it; he will ruin its face and scatter its inhabitants—it will be the same for priest as for people, for master as for servant, for mistress as for maid, for seller as for buyer, for borrower as for lender, for debtor as for creditor. The earth will be completely laid waste and totally plundered. The Lord has spoken this word. The earth dries up and withers, the world languishes and withers, the exalted of the earth languish. The earth is defiled by its people; they have disobeyed the laws, violated the statutes and broken the everlasting covenant.
Therefore a curse consumes the earth its people must bear their guilt, therefore earth's inhabitants are burned up, and very few are left."

"Shirley, I call on the peoples of this earth—come, return to your God that you may be saved." Yes Lord, I pray that they will Listen. *"Yes for I bring warning to all now while there is still time. Return to My Word. Heed My Word. I come soon and I want none to perish."*

The hand of the Lord is heavy and I feel the urgency of the Lord's Words. *"I am that I am. I am coming and I am coming soon. Listen to what I am saying for now is the time."* Lord you are coming and the world is fast asleep. *"Yes, Shirley they sleep because their shepherds do not know the time. Shirley, go to Jude 1:17 – 22,"*

"But, dear friends, remember what the apostles of our Lord Jesus Christ foretold. They said to you, 'In the last times there will be scoffers who will follow their own ungodly desires.' These are the men who divide you, who follow mere natural instincts and do not have the Spirit. But you dear friends, build yourselves up in your most holy faith and pray in the Holy Spirit. Keep yourselves in God's love as you wait for the mercy of our Lord Jesus Christ to bring you to eternal life.
"Be merciful to those who doubt; snatch others from the fire and save them; to others show mercy, mixed with fear—hating even the clothing stained by corrupted flesh." *"Go to 1 John 2:15 – 28,"*

Do Not Love the World.

"Do not love the world or anything in the world. If anyone loves the world, the love of the Father is not in him. For everything in the world—the cravings of sinful man, the lust of his eyes and the boasting of what he has and does—comes not from the Father but from the world. The world and its desires pass away, but the man who does the will of God lives forever.

Warning against Antichrists. "Dear children, this is the last hour; and as you have heard that the antichrist is coming, even now many antichrists have come. This is how we know it is the last hour.

They went out from us, but they did not really belong to us. For if they had belonged to us, they would have remained with us; but their going showed that none of them belonged to us. But you have an anointing from the Holy One, and all of you know the truth. I do not write to you because you do not know the truth, but because you know it and because no lie comes from the truth. Who is the liar? It is the man who denies that Jesus is the Christ. Such a man is the antichrist – he denies the Father and the Son. No one who denies the Son has the Father; whoever acknowledges the Son has the Father also.

"See that what you have heard from the beginning remains in you. If it does, you also will remain in the Son and in the Father. And this is what he promised us—even eternal life. I am writing these things to you about those who are trying to lead you astray. As for you, the anointing you received from him remains in you, and you do not need anyone to teach you. But as his anointing teaches you about all things and as that anointing is real, not counterfeit – just as it has taught you, remain in him."
Children of God. "And now, dear children, continue in him, so that when he appears we may be confident and unashamed before him at his coming."

"Shirley, write down carefully what I say to you." Yes, Lord.
"Go to Ezekiel 36:18 – 36," A Prophecy to the Mountains of Israel

"So I poured out my wrath on them because they had shed blood in the land and because they had defiled it with their idols. I dispersed them among the nations, and they were scattered through the countries. I judged them according to their conduct and their actions. And wherever they went among the nations they profaned my holy name, for it was said of them, 'These are the Lord's people, and yet they had to leave his land.' I had concern for my holy name, which the house of Israel profaned among the nations where they had gone.

"Therefore say to the house of Israel, 'This is what the sovereign Lord says: It is not for your sake, O house of Israel, that I am going to do these things, but for the sake of my holy name, which you have profaned among the nations where you have gone. I will show the holiness of my great name, which has been profaned among the nations, the name you have profaned among them. Then the nations will know that I am the Lord, declares the Sovereign Lord, when I show myself holy through you before their eyes.

"'For I will take you out of the nations; I will gather you from all the countries and bring you back into your own land. I will sprinkle clean water on you, and you will be clean; I will cleanse you from all your impurities and from all your idols. I will give you a new heart and put a new spirit in you; I will remove from you your heart of stone and give you a heart of flesh. And I will put my Spirit in you and move you to follow my decrees and be careful to keep my laws. You will live in the land I gave your forefathers; you will be my people, and I will be your God. I will save you from all your uncleanness. I will call for the grain and make it plentiful and will not bring famine upon you. I will increase the fruit of the trees and the crops of the field, so that you will no longer suffer disgrace among the nations because of famine. Then you will remember your evil ways and wicked deeds, and you will loathe yourselves for your sins and detestable practices. I want you to know that I am not doing this for your sake, declares the Sovereign Lord. Be ashamed and disgraced for your conduct, O house of Israel!

"'This is what the Sovereign Lord says: On the day I cleanse you from all your sins, I will resettle your towns, and the ruins will be rebuilt. The desolate land will be cultivated instead of lying desolate in the sight of all who pass through it. They will say, 'This land that was laid waste has become like the garden of Eden; the cities that were lying in ruins, desolate and destroyed, are now fortified and inhabited.' Then the nations around you that remain will know that I the Lord have rebuilt what was destroyed and have replanted what was desolate. I the Lord have spoken, and I will do it.'"

The anointing falls heavier on me and the Lord says to me:
"Shirley, lift up your eyes to the Lord. I want you to know that you have been called to do this work. Therefore, have no fear." Yes Lord, thank you. *"Now listen carefully."* Yes, Lord.
"See I have fulfilled My Word to the Mountains of Israel. My people have returned to the city. Jerusalem is Mine says the Lord God Almighty. It is Mine. So then, know this—all that is written will be, for My Word is Holy and True. Shirley, go to Ezekiel 38,"

A Prophecy against Gog.

"The word of the Lord came to me; 'Son of man, set your face against Gog, of the land of Magog, the chief prince of Meshech and Tubal; prophesy against him and say; 'This is what the Sovereign Lord says: I am against you, O Gog, chief prince of Meshech and Tubal. I will turn you around, put hooks in your jaws and bring you out with your whole army—your horses, your horsemen fully armed, and a great horde with large and small shields, all of them brandishing their swords. Persia, Cush and Put will be with them, all with shields and helmets, also Gomer with all its troops, and Beth Togarmah from the far north with all its troops—the many nations with you. Get ready; be prepared, you and all the hordes gathered about you, and take command of them.'"

"'After many days you will be called to arms. In future years you will invade a land that has recovered from war, whose people were gathered from many nations to the mountains of Israel, which had long been desolate. They had been brought out from the nations, and now all of them live in safety. '"You and all your troops and the many nations with you will go up, advancing like a storm; you will be like a cloud covering the land.

This is what the Sovereign Lord says: On that day thoughts will come into your mind and you will devise an evil scheme. You will say, 'I will invade the land of unwalled villages; I will attack a peaceful and unsuspecting people—all of them living without walls and without gates and bars. I will plunder and loot and turn my hand against the resettled ruins and the people gathered from the nations, rich in livestock and goods, living at the center of the land.' Sheba and Dedan and the merchants of Tarshish and all her villages will say to you, 'Have you come to plunder? Have you gathered your hordes to loot, to carry off silver and gold, to take away livestock and goods and to seize much plunder?'

"Therefore, son of man, prophesy and say to Gog: This is what the Sovereign Lord says: In that day, when my people Israel are living in safety, will you not take notice of it? You will come from your place in the far north, you and many nations with you, all of them riding on horses, a great horde, a mighty army. You will advance against my people Israel like a cloud that covers the land. In days to come, O Gog, I will bring you against my land, so that the nations may know me when I show myself holy through you before their eyes.'

"This is what the Sovereign Lord days: 'Are you not the one I spoke of in former days by my servants the prophets of Israel? At that time they prophesied for years that I will bring you against them. This is what will happen in that day: When Gog attacks the land of Israel, my hot anger will be aroused,' declares the Sovereign Lord. 'In my zeal and fiery wrath I declare that at that time there shall be a great earthquake in the land of Israel. The fish of the sea and the birds of the air, the beasts of the field, every creature that moves along the ground, and all the people on the face on the earth will tremble at my presence. The mountains will be overturned, the cliffs will crumble and every wall will fall to the ground. I will summon a sword against Gog on all my mountains, declares the Sovereign Lord. Every man's sword will be against his brother.

I will execute judgment upon him with plague and bloodshed; I will pour down torrents of rain, hailstones and burning sulphur on him and on his troops and on the many nations with him. And so I will show my greatness and my holiness, and I will make myself known in the sight of many nations. Then they will know that I am the Lord.'"

"Shirley, write down what I say to you carefully." Yes, Lord.

"I give notice to all those who will hear what the Lord your God is saying to you in these times. Know that I come soon and know that My Word is true and faithful and is never returned empty. All that is written will be, so for your sake I have given this warning. Will you hear My Words? Shirley, I have seen all that you are concerned about. So then, know this, I have kept you apart for Myself." Thank you Lord. *"Yes I have kept you for My work. I called you many years ago and I told you that you have a task to do."* Yes Lord. *"You made a vow to Me to do this task."* Yes, Lord, I did. *"So then, do not fear."* Yes, Lord, I will not fear. *"That is good."* Thank you Lord. *"Let us go forward. Go to Revelation 6,"*

The Seals

"I watched as the lamb opened the first of the seven seals. Then I heard one of the four living creatures say in a voice like thunder, 'Come!' I looked, and there before me was a white horse! Its rider held a bow, and he was given a crown, and he rode out as a conqueror bent on conquest. When the Lamb opened the second seal, I head the second living creature say, 'Come!' Then another horse came out, a fiery red one.

"Its rider was given power to take peace from the earth and to make men slay each other. To him was given a large sword. When the lamb opened the third seal, I heard the third living creature say, 'Come!' I looked and there before me was a black horse! Its rider was holding a pair of scales in his hand. Then I heard what sounded like a voice among the four living creatures, saying, 'A quart of wheat for a day wages, and three quarts of barley for a day's wages and do not damage the oil and the wine.'

"When the Lamb opened the fourth seal, I heard the voice of the fourth living creature say, 'Come!' I looked and there before me was a pale horse! Its rider was named Death, and Hades was following close behind him. They were given power over a fourth of the earth to kill by sword, famine and plague, and by the wild beasts of the earth.

"When he opened the fifth seal, I saw under the altar the souls of those who had been slain because of the word of God and the testimony they had maintained. They called out in a loud voice, 'How long, Sovereign Lord, holy and true, until you judge the inhabitants of the earth and avenge our blood?' Then each of them was given a white robe, and they were told to wait a little longer, until the number of their fellow servants and brothers who were to be killed as they had been was completed.

"I watched as he opened the sixth seal. There was a great earthquake. The sun turned black like sackcloth made of goat hair, the whole moon turned blood red, and the stars in the sky fell to earth, as late figs drop from a fig tree when shaken by a strong wind. The sky receded like a scroll, rolling up, and every mountain and island was removed from its place. Then the kings of the earth, the princes, the generals, the rich, the mighty, and every slave and every free man hid in caves and among the rocks of the mountains. They called to the mountains and the rocks, "Fall on us and hide us from the face of him who sits on the throne and from the wrath of the Lamb! For the great day of their wrath has come, and who can stand?"'

Lord, how sad it is that man has no regard for You. *"Shirley, I came and died on the tree and gave My life for the people of this earth. But they continue to disown Me."* Yes Lord and those that deny You will suffer their fate. *"Shirley, man is on the path to destruction. Only those who hear and see My Words and open the door to their hearts and repent, will be saved. The arrogant will go on to destruction if they deny Me."*

Lord, I remember that scripture when You called out these words—*"Oh Jerusalem, Jerusalem, you who kill the prophets and stone those sent to you, how often I have longed to gather your children together, as a hen gathers her chicks under her wings, but you were not willing."*

"Yes Shirley and now I long to gather all those who are willing to come to Me." Yes, Lord, I can feel Your heart and it pains You that many will not Listen. *"Shirley, I come soon and that great and terrible day draws all the more closer."* How sad Lord that people cannot see You as the Christ? *"Yes Shirley, but many will be saved by this Word. They will understand and repent."* Yes, Lord. *"Shirley, know this—the arrogance of the arrogant will grow stronger and the weak will grow weaker. The arrogant have no regard for the poor. They steal from them all that they can. I laid My life down for those who have been trampled upon by the arrogant. I say to those that have lost hope, come to Me and receive life. From Me you will receive peace that surpasses all understanding. I am waiting for you. Come now while mercy and grace abound. "I am that I am. Whosoever, calls on My Name will be saved. The birth pains have begun. The end days are drawing closer and My call goes out to all. Do not harden your hearts as you will miss the call of the bridegroom. Rather go and fill your lamps with oil so that you may be ready for you do not know the time or the hour."*

"Go to Revelation 1:7,"

"Look, He Is Coming With The Clouds. And every eye will see Him, even those who pierced Him; and all the peoples of the earth will mourn because of Him. So shall it be! Amen."

"I am that I am and I come soon. Prepare yourselves for I will come like a thief in the night for those who are Mine but to those who are not ready, they will see Me coming with the clouds.
Go to Revelation 1:8,"

"I am the Alpha and the Omega," says the Lord God, "who is, and who was, and who is to come, the Almighty."

Thursday, 15 March, 2012, Time: 2:45 p.m.

"Shirley, you have seen correctly. Yes my daughter, so this Word will go into the whole world. It will be available in many languages. It will reach all the way to the ends of the earth. I am doing this, so that no one has an excuse. This work will bring My Word to all that will Listen then they will have no excuse. I speak through My Word and I give Word today for all who have an ear to Listen." Yes Lord. *"Now Shirley go to Galatians 3:10 – 25,"*

"All who rely on observing the law are under a curse, for it is written: 'Cursed is everyone who does not continue to do everything written in the Book of the Law.' Clearly no one is justified before God by the law, because, 'The righteous will live by faith.' The law is not based on faith; on the contrary, 'The man who does these things will live by them.' Christ redeemed us from the curse of the law by becoming a curse for us, for it is written; 'Cursed is everyone who is hung on a tree.' He redeemed us in order that the blessing given to Abraham might come to the Gentiles through Christ Jesus, so that by faith we might receive the promise of the Spirit.

The Law and the Promise. "Brothers, let me take an example from everyday life. Just as no one can set aside or add to a human covenant that has been duly established, so it is in this case. The promises were spoken to Abraham and to his seed. The Scripture does not say 'and to seeds,' meaning many people, but 'and to your seed,' meaning one person, who is Christ.

"What I mean in this: The law, introduced 430 years later, does not set aside the covenant previously established by God and thus do away with the promise. For if the inheritance depends on the law, then it no longer depends on a promise, but God in his grace gave it to Abraham through a promise. What, then, was the purpose of the law? It was added because of transgressions until the Seed to whom the promise referred had come. The law was put into effect through angels by a mediator. A mediator, however, does not represent just one party: but God is one. Is the law, therefore, opposed to the promises of God? Absolutely not! For if the law had been given that could impart life, then righteousness would certainly have come by the law.

"But the scripture declares that the whole world is a prisoner of sin, so that what was promised, being given through faith in Jesus Christ, might be given to those who believe. Before this faith came, we were held prisoner by the law, locked up until faith should be revealed. So the law was put in charge to lead us to Christ that we might be justified by faith. Now that faith has come, we are no longer under the supervision of the law.

Sons of God. "You are all sons of God through faith in Christ Jesus, for all of you who were baptized into Christ have clothed yourselves with Christ. There is neither Jew nor Greek, slave nor free, male nor female, for you are all one in Christ Jesus. If you belong to Christ, then you are Abraham's seed, and heirs according to the promise."

"Shirley, write this down carefully." Yes, Lord. *"See, the promise made to Abraham in regard to the seed was fulfilled. I am the Christ that was promised. I am the one to fulfill this Word. So then, this promise can only be received through faith. It is by faith in Me that fulfills this promise. I am the seed spoken of before the law was given. That is why without faith you cannot please God. Through faith, righteousness came. Faith is without doubt, the righteousness God spoke of, to Abraham. No one comes to the Father without faith in his Son, the Christ, given to the world. Go to Philippians 1:9 -11,*

"And this is my prayer: That your love may abound more and more in knowledge and depth of insight, so that you may be able to discern what is best and may be pure and blameless until the day of Christ, filled with the fruit of righteousness that comes through Jesus Christ— to the glory and praise of God."

"Go to Hebrews 11:1 – 40,"

"Now faith is being sure of what we hope for and certain of what we do not see. This is what the ancients were commended for.
By faith we understand that the universe was formed at God's command, so that what is seen was not made out of what was visible. By faith Abel offered God a better sacrifice than Cain did. By faith he was commended as a righteous man, when God spoke well of his offerings. And by faith he still speaks, even though he is dead. By faith Enoch was taken from this life,

so that he did not experience death; he could not be found, because God had taken him away. For, before he was taken, he was commended as one who pleased God. And without faith it is impossible to please God, because anyone who comes to him must believe that he exists and that he rewards those who earnestly seek him. By faith Noah, when warned about things not yet seen, in holy fear built the ark to save his family. By his faith he condemned the world and became heir of the righteousness that comes by faith.

"By faith Abraham, when called to go to a place he would later receive as his inheritance, obeyed and went, even though he did not know where he was going. By faith he made his home in the promised land like a stranger in a foreign country; he lived in tents, as did Isaac and Jacob, who were heirs with him of the same promise. For he was looking forward, to the city with foundations, whose architect and builder is God.

"By faith Abraham, even though he was past age—and Sarah herself was barren—was enabled to become a father because he considered him faithful who had made the promise. And so from this one man, and he as good as dead, came descendants, as numerous as the stars in the sky and as countless as the sand on the seashore. All these people were still living by faith when they died. They did not receive the things promised; they only saw them and welcomed them from a distance. And they admitted that they were aliens and strangers on earth. People who say such things show that they are looking for a country of their own. If they had been thinking of the country they had left, they would have had opportunity to return. Instead they were longing for a better country—a heavenly one. Therefore God is not ashamed to be called their God, for he has prepared a city for them. By faith Abraham, when God tested him, offered Isaac as a sacrifice.

"He who had received the promises was about to sacrifice his one and only son, even though God had said to him, 'It is through Isaac that your offspring will be reckoned.' Abraham reasoned that God could raise the dead, and figuratively speaking, he did receive Isaac back from death. By faith Isaac blessed Jacob and Esau in regard to their future. By faith Jacob, when he was dying, blessed each of Joseph's sons, and worshiped as he leaned on the top of his staff.

By faith Joseph, when his end was near, spoke about the exodus of the Israelites from Egypt and gave instructions about his bones.

By faith Moses' parents hid him for three months after he was born, because they saw he was no ordinary child, and they were not afraid of the king's edict. "By faith Moses, when he had grown up, refused to be known as the son of Pharaoh's daughter. He chose to be mistreated along with the people of God rather than to enjoy the pleasures of sin for a short time. He regarded disgrace for the sake of Christ as of greater value than the treasures of Egypt, because he was looking ahead to his reward. By faith he left Egypt, not fearing the king's anger; he persevered because he saw him who is invisible. By faith he kept the Passover and the sprinkling of the blood, so that the destroyer of the firstborn would not touch the firstborn of Israel. By faith the people passed through the Red Sea as on dry land; but when the Egyptians tried to do so, they were drowned. By faith the walls of Jericho fell, after the people had marched around them for seven days.

"By faith the prostitute Rahab, because she welcomed the spies, was not killed with those who were disobedient. And what more shall I say? I do not have time to tell about Gideon, Barak, Samson, Jephthah, David, Samuel and the prophets, who through faith conquered kingdoms, administered justice, and gained what was promised; who shut the mouths of lions, quenched the fury of the flames, and escaped the edge of the sword; whose weakness was turned to strength, and who became powerful in battle and routed foreign armies. Women received back their dead, raised to life again. Others were tortured and refused to be released, so that they might gain a better resurrection. Some faced jeers and flogging, while still others were chained and put in prison.

"They were stoned, they were sawed in two; they were put to death by the sword. They went about in sheepskins and goatskins, destitute, persecuted and mistreated – the world was not worthy of them. They wandered in deserts and mountains, and in caves and holes in the ground. These were all commended for their faith, yet none of them received what had been promised. God had planned something better for us so that only together with us would they be made perfect."

"Now go to Hebrews 3:1 -6," Jesus greater than Moses.

"Therefore, holy brothers, who share in the heavenly calling, fix your thoughts on Jesus, the apostle and high priest whom we confess. He was faithful to the one who appointed him, just as Moses was faithful in all God's house. Jesus has been found worthy of greater honor than Moses, just as the builder of a house has greater honor than the house itself. For, every house is built by someone, but God is the builder of everything. Moses was faithful as a servant in all God's house, testifying to what would be said in the future. But Christ is faithful as a Son over God's house. And we are his house, if we hold on to our courage and the hope of which we boast."

"Shirley, Listen carefully. For all fall short of the glory of God. Sin prevents man from receiving the glory of God. Glory is stored up for all those who come to Him in faith and the knowledge that Jesus is Lord of all. Go to 1 Peter 5:10,"

"And the God of all grace, who called you to his eternal glory in Christ, after you have suffered a little while, will himself restore you and make you strong, firm and steadfast. To him be the power for ever and ever. Amen."

Friday, 16 March, 2012, Time: 9:30 a.m.

"Shirley, Listen carefully." Yes, Lord. *"I want you to write this down."* I am ready Lord. *"We will begin with this—Go to Romans 15:18,"*

"I will not venture to speak of anything except what Christ has accomplished through me in leading the Gentiles to obey God by what I have said and done."

"Shirley, this is what I have called you to do." Yes Lord. *"So then, know this—it is Me speaking through you and in you."* Yes Lord. *"Therefore, be careful as you have been to Listen carefully."* Yes Lord I am trying to do this. *"Shirley I am pleased with your obedience."* Thank you Lord. *"I have this Word to say to the Gentiles: I have come to My daughter to bring this Word to you. I call upon you to heed these Words and to seek Me while I may be found. Many of you have never looked for God but now is the time. I call out to those who serve idols and to those who speak to the dead; I say to you come out of that for it will lead to death. I am the Creator and I am the only way to truth. Truth cannot be found in any other way. Satan has set before you many spiritual paths and all will lead to death. I am*

that I am. I am the Way the Truth and the Life. I call on you to know that not all roads lead to God. Not all roads serve the only true God. I have told you that you will find Me on the narrow road that only a few find. The wide road is broad and filled with spiritual snares to trap you.
"Seek Me now while I may be found. I am found only on the narrow road. See I am the gate to the narrow road. Entrance to this road is only found in Me. Go to Matthew 7:7 -8

"Ask and it will be given to you; seek and you will find; knock and the door will be opened to you. For everyone who asks receives; he who seeks finds; and to him who knocks, the door will be opened."

"See I have spoken to you and I have called you and I seek to save you. My Word is the same Yesterday, Today and Forever. I want all to be saved. The time of great change is coming and has begun. Soon freedom of your hands and your tongue will be strangled and you will not have access to My Word as you do now. Come for now is the time. Seek Me while I may be found." "Shirley, I want you to go to Ezekiel 18:4 & 21 – 24,"

"For every living soul belongs to me, the father as well as the son—both alike belong to me. The soul who sins is the one who will die." "But if a wicked man turns away from all the sins he has committed and keeps all my decrees and does what is just and right, he will surely live; he will not die. None of the offences he has committed will be remembered against him. Because of the righteous things he has done, he will live. Do I take any pleasure in the death of the wicked? declares the Sovereign Lord. Rather, am I not pleased when they turn from their ways and live?

"But if a righteous man turns from his righteousness and commits sin and does the same detestable things the wicked man does, will he live? None of the righteous things he has done will be remembered. Because of the unfaithfulness he is guilty of and because of the sins he has committed, he will die."

"Shirley, now write this down carefully." Yes, Lord.
"See, I call all to be saved. I want none to die. If the wicked repent and come to Me, I will accept him and wash away his sins and if he serves Me I will give him eternal life. But if those who are saved, turn away from Me and do evil in My sight he will lose his salvation if he does not come and repent before Me and turn from his sin. Time is short and I want all to be saved. I call on the wicked and the saved that have turned away from Me—come and receive forgiveness. Come in faith for you are not under the law. Come and serve God with all your heart, mind and soul. Come and be cleansed of sin that I may give you a new heart and a new Spirit. "Time is short and I call on all who are saved. Are your lamps full of oil or are they empty? Now is the time to come and receive forgiveness. Now is the time to call upon your Lord. Now is the time to walk away from all sin that leads to death. Come now while mercy and grace abound."
"Shirley, now go to Philippians 4:19,"

"And my God will meet all your needs according to his glorious riches in Christ Jesus."

"Now Shirley, I want you to go to James 5,"

Warning to Rich Oppressors

"Now listen, you rich people, weep and wail because of the misery that is coming upon you. Your wealth has rotted, and moths have eaten yours clothes. Your gold and silver are corroded. Their corrosion will testify against you and eat your flesh like fire. You have hoarded wealth in the last days. Look! The wages you failed to pay the workmen who mowed your fields are crying out against you. The cries of the harvesters have reached the ears of the Lord Almighty. You have lived on earth in luxury and self-indulgence. You have fattened yourselves in the day of slaughter. You have condemned and murdered innocent men who were not opposing you.

Patience in Suffering. "Be patient, then brothers until the Lord's coming. See how the farmer waits for the land to yield its valuable crop and how patient he is for the autumn and spring rains. You too, be patient and stand firm, because the Lord's coming is near. Don't grumble against each other, brothers, or you will be judged. The Judge is standing at the door! Brothers, as an example of patience in the face of suffering, take the prophets who spoke in the name of the Lord. As you know, we consider blessed those who have persevered. You have heard of Job's perseverance and have seen what the Lord finally brought about. The Lord is full of compassion and mercy. Above all brothers, do not swear – not by heaven or by earth or by anything else. Let your 'Yes' be yes, and your 'No,' no, or you will be condemned." A Prayer of Faith. "Is any one of you in trouble? He should pray! Is anyone happy? Let him sing songs of praise. Is any one of you sick? He should call on the elders of the church to pray over him and anoint him with oil in the name of the Lord. And the prayer offered in faith will make the sick person well; the Lord will raise him up. If he has sinned, he will be forgiven. Therefore confess your sins to each other and pray for each other so that you may be healed. The prayer of a righteous man is powerful and effective.

Elijah was a man just like us. He prayed earnestly that it would not rain, and it did not rain on the land for three and a half years. Again he prayed and the heavens gave rain, and the earth produced its crops. My brothers, if one of you should wander from the truth and someone should bring him back, remember this: Whoever turns a sinner from the error of his way will save him from death and cover over a multitude of sins."

"Shirley, write this down carefully." Yes, Lord.
"Do you see that once saved is not a guarantee of salvation?" Yes, Lord and there are other scriptures that also say this. *"Yes, Shirley. I want all My children to look at themselves in the mirror and really examine their lives. For they will then, with a contrite heart identify their sins. This is the reason I have come to say these Words to them lest there will be no surprise for them when the door shuts closed."* Yes Lord, I understand. *"Now please go to Hebrews 12:14 – 29,"*

Warning Against Refusing God

"Make every effort to live in peace with all men and to be holy, without holiness no one will see the Lord. See to it that no one misses the grace of God and that no bitter root grows up to cause trouble and defile many. See that no one is sexually immoral, or is Godless like Esau, who for a single meal sold his inheritance rights as the oldest son. Afterward, as you know, when he wanted to inherit the blessing, he was rejected. He could bring about no change of mind, though he sought the blessing with tears.

You have not come to a mountain that can be touched and that is burning with fire; to darkness, gloom and storm; to a trumpet blast or to such a voice speaking words that those who heard it begged that no further word be spoken to them, because they could not bear what was commanded; 'If even an animal touches the mountain, it must be stoned.' The sight was so terrifying that Moses said, 'I am trembling with fear.'

"But you have come to Mount Zion, to the heavenly Jerusalem, the city of the living God. You have come to thousands upon thousands of angels in joyful assembly, to the church of the firstborn, whose names are written in heaven. You have come to God, the judge of all men, to the spirits of righteous men made perfect, to Jesus the mediator of a new covenant, and to the sprinkled blood that speaks a better word than the blood of Abel. See to it that you do not refuse him who speaks. If they did not escape when they refused him who warned them on earth, how much less will we, if we turn away from him who warns us from heaven?

"At that time his voice shook the earth, but now he has promised, 'Once more I will shake not only the earth but also the heavens.' The words 'once more' indicate the removing of what can be shaken—that is, created things—so that what cannot be shaken may remain. Therefore, since we are receiving a kingdom that cannot be shaken, let us be thankful, and so worship God acceptably with reverence and awe, for our "God is a consuming fire."'

Lord, this is beautifully written. *"Yes, Shirley and it is the true and faithful Word. My children must obey My Word. They must seek holiness."* Yes, Lord. *"Shirley, now go to Hebrews 1 & 2,"*

"In the past God spoke to our forefathers through the prophets at many times and in various ways, but in these last days he has spoken to us by his Son, whom he appointed heir of all things, and through whom he made the universe. The Son is the radiance of God's glory and the exact representation of his being, sustaining all things by his powerful word. After he had provided purification for sins, he sat down at the right hand of the Majesty in heaven. So he became much superior to the angels as the name he has inherited is superior to theirs. For to which of the angels did God ever say, 'You are my Son; today I have become your Father?' Or again, 'I will be his Father, and He will be my Son.' And again, when God brings his firstborn into the world, he says, 'Let all God's angels worship him.' In speaking of the angels he says, 'He makes his angels winds, his servants flames of fire.' But about the Son he says, 'Your throne, O God, will last for ever and ever, and righteousness will be the scepter of your kingdom. You have loved righteousness and hated wickedness; therefore, God, your God, has set you above your companions by anointing you with the oil of joy.'

"He also says, 'In the beginning, O Lord, you laid the foundations of the earth, and the heavens are the work of your hands. They will perish, but you remain; they will all wear out like a garment, You will roll them up like a robe; like a garment they will be changed. But you remain the same, and your years will never end.' "To which of the angels did God ever say, 'Sit at my right hand until I make your enemies a footstool for your feet.' Are not all angels ministering spirits sent to serve those who will inherit salvation?"

"Go to Hebrews 2,"

Warning to Pay Attention

"We must pay more careful attention, therefore, to what we have heard, so that we do not drift away. For if the message spoken by angels was binding, and every violation and disobedience received its just punishment, how shall we escape if we ignore such a great salvation? This salvation, which was first announced by the Lord, was confirmed to us by those who heard him. God also testified to it by signs, wonders and various miracles, and gifts of the Holy Spirit distributed according to his will.

Jesus Made Like His Brothers. "It is not to angels that he has subjected the world to come, about which we are speaking. But there is a place where someone has testified: 'What is man that you are mindful of him, the son of man that you care for him? You made him a little lower than the angels; You crowned him with glory and honor and put everything under his feet. In putting everything under him, God left nothing that is not subject to him. Yet at present we do not see everything subject to him.'

"But we see Jesus, who was made a little lower than the angels, now crowned with glory and honor because he suffered death, so that by the grace of God he might taste death for everyone. In bringing many sons to glory, it was fitting that God, for whom and through whom everything exists, should make the author of their salvation perfect through suffering. Both the one who makes men holy and those who are made holy are of the same family. So Jesus is not ashamed to call them brothers. He says, 'I will declare your name to my brothers; in the presence of the congregation I will sing your praises.' And again he says, 'I will put my trust in him.' And again he says, 'Here am I, and the children God has given to me.'

"Since the children have flesh and blood, he too shared in their humanity so that by his death he might destroy him who holds the power of death—that is, the devil—and free those who all their lives were held in slavery by their fear of death. For surely it is not the angels he helps, but Abraham's descendants.

"For this reason he had to be made like his brothers in every way, in order that he might become a merciful and faithful high priest in service to God, and that he might make atonement for the sins of the people. Because he himself suffered when he was tempted, he is able to help those who are being tempted."

Lord, this is so lovely and it explains so much. *"Yes Shirley it is good that the ones who will read it will understand."* Yes, Lord.

Saturday, 17 March, 2012, Time: 9:00 a.m.

"I have seen your heart and you have seen My heart." Yes Lord, thank you. *"Listen carefully."* Yes, Lord. *"Since the beginning I have told you in My Word that I am coming to judge the world. But man in his mortal mind has chosen to disregard My Word and turn to evil. This world has become like Sodom and Gomorrah in every way. It has fallen into the depths of sin. Man has become arrogant and disobedient in all that he once believed in. Nations were founded on My Word. People respected God and themselves. But now they respect neither God nor themselves. They live only for sin. This is My warning to all—even the arrogant. I am coming soon and to those who will Listen I say, come out of your sinful ways and begin to respect your bodies and respect the God who made them. You are a disgrace before the eyes of God. You who are on the wide road that leads to destruction. Shirley, go to Romans 1:29 – 32,"*
"They have become filled with every kind of wickedness, evil, greed and depravity. They are full of envy, murder, strife, deceit and malice. They are gossips, slanderers, God-haters,

insolent, arrogant and boastful; they invent ways of doing evil; they disobey their parents; they are senseless, faithless, heartless, ruthless.
Although they know God's righteous decree that those who do such things deserve death, they not only continue to do these very things but also approve of those who practice them."

Lord, I feel You are angry. *"Yes Shirley, after all, I came and paid the price for sin so that they may receive forgiveness and turn away from death."* Lord, the world has no morals. *"Yes Shirley and it is because they have disregarded the One who created them. They have lost their way and fallen into the very depths of sin."* Yes, Lord it is true. *"Shirley, now go to Romans 15:15–16 & 21,"*

Paul the Minister to the Gentiles

"I have written you quite boldly on some points, as if to remind you of them again, because of the grace God gave me to be a minister of Christ Jesus to the Gentiles with the priestly duty of proclaiming the gospel of God, so that the Gentiles might become an offering acceptable to God, sanctified by the holy Spirit. Rather, as it is written: 'Those who were not told about him will see, and those who have not heard will understand.'

*"Shirley, write this down. All who are in trouble, come to Me and surrender your hearts to Me that I may hear you and rescue you. Come and let Me give you, life, for **I am the life**. All you that are lost come to Me and surrender your hearts to Me that I may hear and rescue you. Come for **I am the Way**. All you who are in the world of Babylon, serving other gods, come to Me and surrender your hearts that I may hear you, come to Me for **I am the Truth**. Come now while mercy and grace abound."* *"Go to Psalm 100,"*

"Shout for joy to the Lord, all the earth. Worship the Lord with gladness: come before him with joyful songs. Know that the Lord is God, it is he who made us, and we are his; we are his people, the sheep of his pasture.

"Enter his gates with thanksgiving and his courts with praise; give thanks to him and praise his name. For the Lord is good and his love endures forever; his faithfulness continues through all generations."

Sunday, 18 March, 2012, Time: 12:20 p.m.

"Shirley, Listen carefully." Yes, Lord. *"Go to John 14:8 – 31,"*

Jesus Speaking

"Philip said, 'Lord, show us the Father and that will be enough for us.' Jesus answered: 'Don't you know me, Philip, even after I have been among you such a long time? Anyone who has seen me has seen the Father. How can you say, 'Show us the Father'? Don't you believe that I am in the Father, and that the Father is in me? The words I say to you are not just my own. Rather, it is the Father, living in me, who is doing his work. Believe me when I say that I am in the Father and the Father is in me; or at least believe on the evidence of the miracles themselves.

"'I tell you the truth, anyone who has faith in me will do what I have been doing. He will do even greater than these, because I am going to the Father. And I will do whatever you ask in my name, so that the Son may bring glory to the Father. You may ask me for anything in my name, and I will do it.'

"Jesus Promises the Holy Spirit. 'If you love me, you will obey what I command. And I will ask the Father, and he will give you another Counselor to be with you forever—the Spirit of Truth. The world cannot accept him, because it neither sees him nor knows him. But you know, for he lives with you and will be in you. I will not leave you as orphans; I will come to you. Before long, the world will not see me anymore, but you will see me. Because I live, you also will live. On that day you will realize that I am in my Father, and you are in me, and I am in you. Whoever has my commands and obeys them, he is the one who loves me. He who loves me will be loved by my father, and I too will love him and show myself to him.'

"Then Judas (not Judas Iscariot) said, 'But Lord, why do you intend to show yourself to us and not to the world?' Jesus replied, 'If anyone loves me, he will obey my teaching. My Father will love him and we will come to him and make our home with him. He who does not love me will not obey my teaching. These words you hear are not my own; they belong to the father who sent me. All this I have spoken while still with you. But the Counselor, the Holy Spirit, whom the Father will send in my name, will teach you all things and will remind you of everything I have said to you.

"Peace I leave with you; my peace I give you. I do not give to you as the world gives. Do not let your hearts be troubled and do not be afraid. You heard me say, 'I am going away and I am coming back to you.' If you loved me, you would be glad that I am going to the Father, for the Father is greater than I.
I have told you now before it happens, so that when it does happen you will believe.' "I will not speak with you much longer, for the prince of this world is coming. He has no hold on me, but the world must learn that I love the Father and that I do exactly what my Father has commanded me.'"

"Now Listen to Me and write down what I tell you Word for Word." Yes, Lord. "See I am in the Father and the Father is in Me as I am in you. No one comes to the Father but by Me. I am the Way, the Truth and the Life. All who know Me know My Father. I came so that the will of the Father will be done on earth as it is done in heaven. Now all who come to Me, come to the Father. Now Shirley go to Genesis 1:1 – 31,"

"In the beginning God created the heavens and the earth. Now the earth was formless and empty, darkness was over the surface of the deep, and the Spirit of God was hovering over the waters. And God said, 'Let there be light,' and there was light. God saw that the light was good, and he separated the light from the darkness. God called the light 'day,' and the darkness he called 'night.'

"And there was evening, and there was morning—the first day. And God said, 'Let there be an expanse between the waters to separate water from water.' So God made the expanse and separated the water under the expanse from the water above it. And it was so. God called the expanse 'sky.' And there was evening, and there was morning—the second day. "And God said, 'Let the water under the sky be gathered to one place and let dry ground appear.' And it was so. God called the dry ground 'land,' and the gathered waters he called 'seas.' And God saw that is was good. Then God said, 'Let the land produce vegetation: seed-bearing, plants and trees on the land that bear fruit with seed in it, according to their various kinds.' And it was so. The land produced vegetation: plants bearing seed according to their kinds and trees bearing fruit with seed in it according to their kinds.

And God saw that it was good. And there was evening, and there was morning—the third day. "And God said, 'Let there be lights in the expanse of the sky to separate the day from the night, and let them serve as signs to mark seasons and days and years, and let them be lights in the expanse of the sky to give light on the earth.' And it was so. God made two great lights – the greater light to govern the day and the lesser light to govern the night. He also made the stars. God set them in the expanse of the sky to give light on the earth, to govern the day and the night, and to separate light from darkness. And God saw that is was good. And there was evening, and there was morning—the fourth day. "And God said, 'Let the water teem with living creatures, and let birds fly above the earth across the expanse of the sky.' So God created the great creatures of the sea and every living and moving thing, with which the water teems, according to their kind, and every winged bird according to its kind. And God saw that it was good. God blessed them and said, 'Be fruitful and increase in number and fill the water in the seas, and let the birds increase on the earth.' And there was evening, and there was morning—the fifth day. "And God said, 'Let the land produce living creatures according to their kinds: livestock, creatures that move along the ground, and wild animals, each according to its kind.' And it was so. God made the wild animals according to their kinds, the livestock according to their kinds, and all the creatures that move along the ground according to their kinds. And God saw that it was good. Then God said, 'Let us make man in our image, in our likeness, and let them rule over the fish of the sea and the birds of the air, over the livestock, over all the earth, and over all the creatures that move along the ground.' So God created man in his own image, in the image of God he created him; male and female he created them.

"God blessed them and said to them, 'Be fruitful and increase in number; fill the earth and subdue it. Rule over the fish of the sea and the birds of the air and over every living creature that moves on the ground.' Then God said, 'I give you every seed-bearing plant on the face of the whole earth and every tree that has fruit with seed in it. They will be yours for food. And to all the beasts of the earth and all the birds of the air and all the creatures that move on the ground—everything that has the breath of life in it—I give every green plant for food, and it was so. God saw all that he had made, and it was very good. And there was evening, and there was morning—the sixth day."

Monday, 19 March, 2012, Time: 8:50 a.m.

"Shirley, Listen carefully." Yes, Lord. *"Since the beginning of time the world was created by My Word. I spoke and it came into being. I am the Word that became flesh and walked among you. Therefore, I am the Creator. Man in his own mind has tried to dishonor My Name and My work but I am that I am. All living things on this earth are done by My Hand and by My Word.*

"I am the Beginning and the End. All has been created by Me and none other. I am the Creator and this is My Creation and so be it. Those that choose to believe that I am not the Creator are the arrogant. They are blind and they cannot see My Hand. I am God of all and there is none other.

"I come to tell you this, in this Word and by My Word so that there is no excuse. I come to give this Word and by My Word so that the arrogant will know that I have spoken. This Word that I write now is for all those who deny My Creation and therefore deny Me. I am that I am. See to it that you are not fooled by those who deny the Work of My Hand and My Word. For if you deny Me you deny the Father. If you deny Me I will deny you before the Father. I have come to give this Word to confirm My Word and the Word in the Bible. If you deny My Word and the Word of the Bible you deny Me. I come to give this warning to all who will hear what I am saying—this is a warning to you. You will have no excuse. My Creation, on its own, is proof of My Hand. If you deny My Creation you deny Me! Shirley, go to John 1:1 – 18,"

"In the beginning was the Word, and the Word was with God, and the Word was God. He was with God in the beginning. Through him all things were made; without him nothing was made that has been made. In him was life, and that life was the light of men. The light shines in the darkness, but the darkness has not understood it.

There came a man who was sent from God; his name was John. He came as a witness to testify concerning that light, so that through him all men might believe. He himself was not the light; he came only as a witness to the light. The true light that gives light to every man was coming into the world.

"He was in the world, and though the world was made through him, the world did not recognize him. He came to that which was his own, but his own did not receive him. Yet to all who received him, to those who believed in his name, he gave the right to become children of God—children born not of natural descent, nor of human decision or a husband's will, but born of God.
"The Word became flesh and made his dwelling among us. We have seen his glory, the glory of the One and Only, who came from the Father, full of grace and truth. John testifies concerning him. He cries out, saying, 'This was he of whom I said, "He who comes after me has surpassed me because he was before me."'

"From the fullness of his grace we have all received one blessing after another. For the law was given through Moses; grace and truth came through Jesus Christ. No one has ever seen God, but God the One and Only, who is at the Father's side, has made him known."
Lord, this is beautifully explained. *"Yes Shirley. John was a great man—he came and prepared the way for Me."* Yes, Lord. *"Shirley, go to John 18:28 – 40,"*

Jesus before Pilate

"Then the Jews led Jesus from Caiaphas to the palace of the Roman governor. By now it was early morning, and to avoid ceremonial uncleanness the Jews did not enter the palace; they wanted to be able to eat the Passover. So Pilate came out to them and asked, 'What charges are you bringing against this man?' 'If he were not a criminal,' they replied, 'we would not have handed him over to you.' Pilate said, 'Take him yourselves and judge him by your own law.' 'But we have no right to execute anyone,' the Jews objected.

"This happened so the words Jesus had spoken indicating the kind of death he was going to die would be fulfilled. Pilate then went back inside the palace, summoned Jesus and asked him, 'Are you the king of the Jews?' 'Is that your own idea,' Jesus asked, 'or did others talk to you about me?' 'Am I a Jew?' Pilate replied, 'It was your people and your chief priests who handed you over to me. What is it you have done?'

"Jesus said, 'My kingdom is not of this world. If it were, my servants would fight to prevent my arrest by the Jews. But now my kingdom is from another place.' 'You are a king then!' said Pilate.

Jesus answered, 'You are right in saying I am a King. In fact, for this reason I was born, and for this I came into the world, to testify to the truth. Everyone on the side of truth listens to me.' '"What is the truth?' Pilate asked. With this he went out again to the Jews and said, 'I find no basis for a charge against him. But it is your custom for me to release to you one prisoner at the time of the Passover. Do you want me to release "The King of the Jews?"' They shouted back, 'No, not him! Give us Barabbas!' Now Barabbas had taken part in a rebellion.

"Go to John 19:6 – 16,"

Jesus Sentenced To Be Crucified

"As soon as the chief priests and their officials saw him, they shouted, 'Crucify! Crucify!' But Pilate answered, 'You take him and crucify him. As for me, I find no basis for a charge against him.' The Jews insisted, 'We have a law, and according to that law he must die, because he claimed to be the Son of God.'

"When Pilate heard this he was even more afraid, and he went back inside the palace. 'Where do you come from?' He asked Jesus, but Jesus gave him no answer. 'Do you refuse to speak to me?' Pilate said. 'Don't you realize I have power either to free you or to crucify you?' "Jesus answered, 'You would have no power over me if it were not given to you from above. Therefore the one who handed me over to you is guilty of a greater sin.' From then on, Pilate tried to set Jesus free, but the Jews kept shouting, 'If you let this man go, you are no friend of Caesar. Anyone who claims to be a king opposes Caesar.'

When Pilate heard this, he brought Jesus out and sat down on the judge's seat at a place known as the Stone Pavement (which in Aramaic is Gabbatha). It was the day of Preparation of Passover Week, about the sixth hour. 'Here is your king,' Pilate said to the Jews. But they shouted, 'Take him away! Take him away! Crucify him!' 'Shall I crucify your king?' Pilate asked. 'We have no king but Caesar,' the chief priests answered. Finally Pilate handed him over to them to be crucified."

"Go to John 19:19 – 24,

The Crucifixion

"Pilate had a notice prepared and fastened to the cross. It read:
JESUS OF NAZARETH, THE KING OF THE JEWS. Many of the Jews read this sign, for the place where Jesus was crucified was near the city, and the sign was written in Aramaic, Latin and Greek. The chief priests of the Jews protested to Pilate, 'Do not write "The King of the Jews", but that this man claimed to be king of the Jews.'" Pilate answered, 'What I have written, I have written.'

"When the soldiers crucified Jesus, they took his clothes, dividing them into four shares, one for each of them, with the undergarment remaining. This garment was seamless, woven in

one piece from top to bottom. 'Let's not tear it,' they said to one another. 'Let's decide by lot who will get it.'
"This happened that the scripture might be fulfilled which said, 'They divided my garments among them and cast lots for my clothing.' So this is what the soldiers did."
"Go to John 19:28 – 30 & 33 – 42, The Death of Jesus.

"Later, knowing that all was now completed, and so that scripture would be fulfilled, Jesus said, 'I am thirsty.' A jar of wine vinegar was there, so they soaked a sponge in it, put the sponge on a stalk of the hyssop plant, and lifted it to Jesus' lips. When he had received the drink, Jesus said, 'It is finished.' With that, he bowed his head and gave up his spirit. But when they came to Jesus and found he was already dead, they did not break his legs. Instead, one of the soldiers pierced Jesus' side with a spear, bringing a sudden flow of blood and water.

"The man who saw it has given testimony, and his testimony is true. He knows he tells the truth, and he testifies so that you may believe.
These things happened so that the scripture would be fulfilled;
'Not one of his bones will be broken,' and, as another scripture says, 'They will look on the One they have pierced.'"

The Burial of Jesus

"Later, Joseph of Arimathea asked Pilate for the body of Jesus. Now Joseph was a disciple of Jesus, but secretly because he feared the Jews. With Pilate's permission, he came and took the body away. He was accompanied by Nicodemus, the man who earlier had visited Jesus at night. Nicodemus brought a mixture of myrrh and aloes, about seventy-five pounds. Taking Jesus' body, the two of them wrapped it, with spices, in strips of linen. This was in accordance with Jewish burial customs. At the place where Jesus was crucified, there was a garden, and in the garden a new tomb, in which no one had ever been laid.
Because it was the Jewish day of Preparation and since the tomb was nearby, they laid Jesus there."

"Go to John 20:1 – 9,

The Empty Tomb

"Early on the first day of the week, while it was still dark, Mary Magdalene went to the tomb and saw that the stone had been removed from the entrance. So she came running to Simon Peter and the other disciple, the one Jesus loved, and said, 'They have taken the Lord out of the tomb, and we don't know where they have put him!' So Peter and the other disciple started for the tomb. Both were running, but the other disciple outran Peter and reached the tomb first. He bent over and looked in at the strips of linen lying there but did not go in. Then Simon Peter, who was behind him, arrived and went into the tomb. He saw the strips of linen lying there, as well as the burial cloth that had been around Jesus' head. The cloth was folded up by itself, separate from the linen. Finally the other disciple, who had reached the tomb first, also went inside. He saw and believed. (They still did not understand from Scripture that Jesus had to rise from the dead.)"

"Write this down carefully." Yes, Lord. *"See, I came down to earth that you may have life. See I am that I am. Before Abraham, I am. Now that you have seen, will you believe? Will*

you understand? My Word has gone into the whole world and many have chosen to ignore it. You will not see Me until I come again. On that day many will know that I am that I am. Now, Shirley." Yes, Lord. *"Go to Isaiah 55:11,"*

"So is my word that goes out from my mouth: it will not return to me empty, but will accomplish what I desire and achieve the purpose for which I sent it."
"Shirley, go to Daniel 9:20 – 27,"

The Seventy "Sevens"

"While I was speaking and praying, confessing my sin and the sin of my people Israel and making my request to the Lord my God for his holy hill – while I was still in prayer, Gabriel, the man I had seen in the earlier vision, came to me in swift flight about the time of the evening sacrifice. He instructed me and said to me, 'Daniel, I have now come to give you insight and understanding. As soon as you began to pray, an answer was given, which I have come to tell you, for you are highly esteemed. Therefore, consider the message and understand the vision: seventy 'sevens' are decreed for your people and your holy city to finish transgression, to put an end to sin, to atone for wickedness, to bring in everlasting righteousness, to seal up vision and prophecy and to anoint the most holy. Know and understand this: from the issuing of the decree to restore and rebuild Jerusalem until the Anointed One, the ruler, comes, there will be seven 'sevens,' and sixty-two 'sevens.' It will be rebuilt with streets and a trench, but in times of trouble. After the sixty-two 'sevens,' the Anointed One will be cut off and will have nothing. The people of the ruler who will come will destroy the city and the sanctuary.

"The end will come like a flood: war will continue until the end, and desolations have been decreed. He will confirm a covenant with many for one 'seven.' In the middle of the 'seven' he will put an end to sacrifice and offering. And on a wing of the temple, he will set up an abomination that causes desolation, until the end that is decreed is poured out on him.'"

"Shirley, write this down carefully." Yes, Lord. *"This is the time of the beginning of the great tribulation that has been spoken of in the Word. See to it that you stay awake for you know not the hour that I will come. Shirley, I have given you this Word to bring to the people because many do not believe that I am coming back soon."* Soon, Lord? *"Yes soon."*

"Now Shirley, Listen carefully." Yes, Lord. The anointing falls heavier on me.

"All that accept this Word as truth will be set free. Those that will not and remain stubborn will find themselves shut out of the kingdom to come. I have given this Word as a warning to those that will Listen. But those who deny this Word will deny Me. I have set this work to be a Word spoken by My mouth to My servant and if you choose to deny this then you will deny Me. Time is short and I want all to be saved. Hear what the Lord your God is saying to you this day.

"Shirley, you have been prepared to do this. You have suffered contempt by many that have slandered your name. But I have chosen you to do this for Me as you have proven yourself faithful. You have stood strong even when you have heard your name being slandered. They scoff at the work you have done. Do they not know that I was the One that gave you that work to do?"

Yes, Lord that is why I ignore their remarks. *"Shirley, many will not accept this Work. But know this—I have warned you before time."* Yes, Lord, thank you as that is all I need to stand strong.

Tuesday, 20 March, 2012, Time: 1:25 p.m.

"Shirley, write this down carefully." Yes, Lord.
"Go to 2 Thessalonians 2: 1 – 12,"

The Man of Lawlessness

"Concerning the coming of our Lord Jesus Christ and our being gathered to him, we ask you, brothers, not to become easily unsettled or alarmed by some prophecy, report or letter supposed to have come from us, saying that the day of the Lord has already come. Don't let anyone deceive you in any way for that day will not come until the rebellion occurs and the man of lawlessness is revealed, the man doomed to destruction.

"He will oppose and will exalt himself over everything that is called God or is worshiped, so that he sets himself up in God's temple proclaiming himself to be God. Don't you remember that when I was with you I used to tell you these things? And now you know what is holding him back, so that he may be revealed at the proper time. For the secret power of lawlessness is already at work; but the one who now holds it back will continue to do so till he is taken out of the way. And then the lawlessness one will be revealed whom the Lord Jesus will overthrow with the breath of his mouth and destroy by the splendor of his coming.

"The coming of the lawless one will be in accordance with the work of Satan displayed in all kinds of counterfeit miracles, signs and wonders, and in every sort of evil that deceives those who are perishing. They perish because they refused to love the truth and so be saved. For this reason God sends them a powerful delusion so that they will believe the lie and so that all will be condemned who have not believed the truth but have delighted in wickedness.

"Shirley, write this down carefully." Yes, Lord.
"The lawlessness of the lawless one will prevail upon the earth. Only the wise will understand. The foolish will be left and be deceived. This is coming as has in fact already begun and the wise will see and know. Therefore, stand ready and be alert for you know not the hour or the day that the Lord will come. Only those who are awake and wise will see Me. This is a warning to those who choose to hear the Words I speak. To those who remain foolish, you will be deceived. Now is the time to come while grace and mercy abound. Shirley, go to Isaiah 25,"

Praise the Lord

"O Lord, you are my God; I will exalt you and praise your name, for in perfect faithfulness you have done marvelous things, things planned long ago. You have made the city a heap of rubble, the fortified town a ruin, the foreigner's stronghold a city no more; it will never be rebuilt. Therefore strong peoples will honor you; cities of ruthless nations will revere you.

"You have been a refuge for the poor, a refuge for the needy in his distress, a shelter from the storm and a shade from the heat. For the breath of the ruthless is like a storm driving against a wall and like the heat of the desert. You silence the uproar of foreigners; as heat is reduced by the shadow of a cloud, so the song of the ruthless is stilled.

"On this mountain the Lord Almighty will prepare a feast of rich food for all peoples, a banquet of aged wine – the best of meats and the finest of wines. On this mountain he will destroy the shroud that enfolds all peoples, the sheet that covers all nations; he will swallow up death forever.

"The Sovereign Lord will wipe away the tears from all faces; he will remove the disgrace of his people from all the earth. The Lord has spoken. 'In that day they will say, "Surely this is our God; we trusted in him, and he saved us. This is the Lord we trusted in him; let us rejoice and be glad in his salvation."'

"The hand of the Lord will rest on this mountain; but Moab will be trampled under him as straw is trampled down in the manure. They will spread out their hands in it, as a swimmer spreads out his hands to swim. God will bring down their pride despite the cleverness of their hands. He will bring down your high fortified walls and lay them low; He will bring them down to the ground, to the very dust."

"Shirley, I want you to Listen carefully." Yes, Lord.
"I have this to say to the churches: 'Prepare your sheep, you shepherds. Prepare them to be ready for the coming of their Lord. Many of My sheep have been scattered and some have lost their way. Go and find the lost sheep and bring them into the pasture that they may be fed. I am telling you this now so that My sheep may be ready. Keep them and feed them the True Word and do not allow your church to become a circus.'

"Now is the time to become serious with the Word. My Word must be in the hearts of My sheep. They must understand the Word and what the cost is to follow Me. They must understand that My Way is Holy. They must understand that the path is narrow and the journey they are called to travel is a holy one. They must understand that sin leads to death. They must understand that I am Holy.

*"Through Me, they receive life. Tell them that My sheep know My voice and they must seek Me with a contrite heart and they will find Me. I am here waiting to come into the hearts of those who will come. I died for their sin. I want all to be saved and none to be lost. Come, gather your sheep and prepare for Me. I come for a spotless and blameless bride. Come now, while mercy and grace abound. Come now for **now** is the time. Make straight the path of the Lord. Shirley, go to Revelation 20:4 – 6,*

"I saw the thrones on which were seated those who had been given authority to judge. And I saw the souls of those who had been beheaded because of their testimony for Jesus and because of the word of God. They had not worshiped the beast or his image and had not received his mark on their foreheads or their hands. They came to life and reigned with Christ a thousand years."

"Write this down carefully." Yes, Lord. *"See a time of great tribulation is coming upon this world. Now is the time for those who come to Me, to stand strong. Faith will be challenged. Only those who prove faithful will see the Lord. Do not be deceived, for deception will*

overflow and those who stand firm in their faith in Me will stand. See I have warned you before the time that there is no excuse. My Word is My Word.

"I call you now to Listen to what I am saying to the church. Time is short and now is the time to prepare your hearts and stand in Me and with Me. For I am your High Priest, the Christ. Go to Ephesians 6:10 – 18,"

The Armor of God

"Finally, be strong in the Lord and in his mighty power. Put on the full armor of God so that you can take your stand against the devil's schemes. For our struggle is not against flesh and blood, but against the rulers, against the authorities, against the powers of this dark world and against the spiritual forces of evil in the heavenly realms.

"Therefore put on the full armor of God, so that when the day of evil comes, you may be able to stand your ground, and after you have done everything, to stand. Stand firm then, with the belt of truth buckled around your waist, with the breastplate of righteousness in place, and with your feet fitted with the readiness that comes from the gospel of peace.

"In addition, to all this, take up the shield of faith, with which you can extinguish all the flaming arrows of the evil one. Take the helmet of salvation and the sword of the Spirit, which is the word of God. And pray in the Spirit on all occasions with all kinds of prayers and requests. With this in mind, be alert and always keep on praying for all the saints."

"Yes, My children, now is the time to prepare for war. Prepare now as the world heads down its path of destiny. Keep in mind, always, that I come soon, sooner than many believe. Keep in mind that I love you and that I want all to be saved. Keep in mind that I have made the road open before you. "All of heaven is waiting for you. Just, come and join the battle so that you will be saved so that you will see the glory of God."

"Shirley, go to Psalm 121,"

"I lift up my eyes to the hills—where does my help come from?
My help comes from the Lord, the maker of heaven and earth.
He will not let your foot slip—He who watches over you will not slumber; indeed, he who watches over Israel will neither slumber nor sleep. The Lord watches over you—the Lord is your shade at
your right hand. The sun will not harm you by day, nor the moon by night.
"The Lord will keep you from all harm—He will watch over your life; the Lord will watch over your coming and going both now and forevermore."

"This work is complete." Yes, Lord, thank you.

"Shirley, you are blessed. Do not fear." Thank you Lord.

"Shirley, I have given you this work to do for Me, to bring into the world. So then you must understand that many will come against you but do not fear as I have given you this to do. I am about to tell you so listen carefully." I have done this as a warning to the world as they

have turned away from Me. I do nothing until I tell My prophets. I have taught you over the years to hear My word and you will be called to stand accountable for them, the Words. Will you do this?" Yes, Lord.

For those who have back slidden or luke-warm, ***repent*** and return to Jesus and for those readers that have not given their lives to Jesus – Come now is the time – the time of grace and mercy. Do not ignore this warning from the Lord. Please humble yourselves and acknowledge that you are sinners. Come now is the time to come to hear His voice. Just pray this prayer out loud and make Jesus the Lord of your lives.

Heavenly Father,

I hear Your voice and I feel Your knock on the door to my heart. I come in humbleness before You Father and I thank You for sending Your Son, Jesus to die on the cross for me.

I admit and that I am a sinner and I repent for my sin and ask You to forgive me and wash me clean of sin and guilt.

I confess with my mouth that Jesus Christ is Lord and I believe in my heart that God raised Him from the dead according to Romans 10: 9 & 10.

I open the door and invite You in. I receive You now into my heart. Come in Lord Jesus and I make You the Lord of my life. I ask You to lead me from this day forward not my will but Your will. I will serve You and obey You all the days of my life. Thank You that by Your blood I am saved.

In Jesus Name

Amen

You have just made the most important decision of your life and are now spiritually born and your sins have been forgiven. Your new life in Christ Jesus has begun.

John 1: 12-13

Yet to all who received Him, to those who believed on His name, He gave the right to become children of God – children born not of natural descent, nor of human decision or a husband's will, but born of God.

Romans 8: 11
And if the Spirit of Him who raised Jesus from the dead is living in you, He who raised Christ from the dead will also give life to your mortal bodies through His Spirit, who lives in you.

Romans 5: 1-2
Therefore, since we have been justified through faith, we have peace with God through our Lord Jesus Christ, through whom we gained access by faith into this grace in which we now stand.

Always remember that your salvation did not come cheap – it was willingly paid for by the blood of Christ. You are 'saved' - there is no other way into heaven so Jesus is never shared with any other god. We no longer live under the law but have been set free in Christ through grace and faith. All roads do not lead to heaven. Do not abuse the grace of God as it is not a licence to sin.

Remember that sin separates man from God. So make a decision in your life, to turn away from sin that you may be in. Remember too that Jesus is coming for a pure and blameless bride so set out from this day forward to seek holiness. By faith you accepted Christ as Lord so build on this faith to run the race of life and stand in faith against every trial and tribulation because the Lord said in this word that we will need faith to stand as we continue in the birth pains of His soon return. Look up towards heaven as we eagerly wait for His soon coming. Come out of the world. We are in the final hours.

Love, respect and honour God because He loves, respects and honours you and always give God all the praise, honour and glory for He alone is worthy. Seek holiness! The Lord is seeking all to hear His voice therefore, strive towards a close and personal relationship with the Lord by spending time in prayer each day and in the Bible for the Holy Spirit to teach you to be able to **Hear His Voice**!

www.ingramcontent.com/pod-product-compliance
Lightning Source LLC
Chambersburg PA
CBHW071417040426
42445CB00012BA/1186